Jesus Among Giants

This book is part of the Peter Lang Humanities list.
Every volume is peer reviewed and meets
the highest quality standards for content and production.

PETER LANG
New York • Bern • Berlin
Brussels • Vienna • Oxford • Warsaw

William Cully Allen

Jesus Among Giants

Religious Biographies in Comparative Context

PETER LANG
New York • Bern • Berlin
Brussels • Vienna • Oxford • Warsaw

Library of Congress Cataloging-in-Publication Data
Names: Allen, William Cully, author.
Title: Jesus among giants: religious biographies in comparative context /
William Cully Allen.
Description: New York: Peter Lang, 2019.
Includes bibliographical references and index.
Identifiers: LCCN 2019022507 | ISBN 978-1-4331-6628-0 (hardback: alk. paper)
ISBN 978-1-4331-6629-7 (ebook pdf) | ISBN 978-1-4331-6630-3 (epub)
ISBN 978-1-4331-6631-0 (mobi)
Subjects: LCSH: Christianity and other religions. | Religions.
Religious Leaders—Biography.
Classification: LCC BR127 .A45 2019 | DDC 206/.3—dc23
LC record available at https://lccn.loc.gov/2019022507
DOI 10.3726/b15255

Bibliographic information published by **Die Deutsche Nationalbibliothek**.
Die Deutsche Nationalbibliothek lists this publication in the "Deutsche
Nationalbibliografie"; detailed bibliographic data are available
on the Internet at http://dnb.d-nb.de/.

The paper in this book meets the guidelines for permanence and durability
of the Committee on Production Guidelines for Book Longevity
of the Council of Library Resources.

Printed in the United States of America

CONTENTS

ACKNOWLEDGMENTS

Forty years ago I took a seminar at Gordon-Conwell Theological Seminary that would eventually lead me to write this book. Professor Lit-Sen Chang conducted a missions seminar called "Christian Approach to Asian Religions." After having been a Confucian scholar, Daoist philosopher and Zen Buddhist master, Professor Chang was converted to faith in Jesus. He related to the class how he was en route from China to India on a missionary campaign to propagate Zen Buddhism when, during a layover in the Philippines, he was taken reluctantly to a Christian church, heard the gospel for the first time, and was immediately converted to faith. He taught us how to recognize common ground between Jesus and Asian religions as a point of departure for dialogue and declaration of the gospel.

I am indebted to the late Srinarayanmisra of Banāras Hindu University for teaching me how to navigate Hindu and Buddhist philosophical literature, to the late Charles Wei-Hsen Fu of Temple University for teaching me how to read Confucian and Daoist texts in their comparative philosophical contexts, and to my late PhD advisor, Bibhuti Singh Yadav, for training me how to think—in the face of opponents—through sacred texts in comparative religious contexts.

Colleagues, friends, and family have helped to render an otherwise difficult discourse far more reader-friendly by offering their constructive comments, criticisms, and corrections: Tim Clark, Howard Shultz, Stephen Inbanathan, Jagannatha Charan Das, Daniel Kremer, Kevin Borella, and Cynthia, Gabriel, Emma, Richard and Russell Allen. Peter Lang editor, Liam McLean masterfully mediated an invaluable peer review of a preliminary draft, and Luke McCord meticulously prepared the manuscript for publication. I am especially grateful to Meagan Simpson for her confidence in the project's contribution. The cover design is the creation and contribution of Carla Strozzieri. Reading from left to right and top to bottom, the symbols signify Hinduism, Buddhism, Islam, Confucianism, Christianity, Daoism, Judaism and Jainism respectively.

INTRODUCTION

"Out in the open, wisdom calls aloud, she raises her voice in the public square."[1]

There are several competing approaches for comparing foundational religious figures. First, there are scholars belonging to each religion who insist that theirs is the best, better than all the rest. They acknowledge valid insights of other foundational religious figures but simply claim that theirs taught or accomplished something more important than all the others.[2] A particular problem with this perspective is the difficulty in establishing a common criteria on the basis of which to objectively evaluate and determine who is superior.

A second approach denies that any single religious figure is superior but claims instead that all of them say essentially the same thing in different words to different people in different historical situations. Scholars who take this approach marginalize and minimize differences and claim that all teach a common core message. All religious roads lead to the same destination and all different kinds of people reach there.[3] This position is difficult to defend because there is no consensus concerning the core message that they all allegedly share in common. Moreover, the many conflicting truth claims concerning life's ultimate goal and the means for reaching it are not readily reconcilable.

A third approach begs to differ with the previous two by denying both the superiority of any one foundational figure and the essential similarity of them all. No one has a monopoly on the market of religious truth, but each one contributes their own particular perspectives on truth which transcends them all. In light of conflicting assertions, this approach claims that each spiritual giant taught some truth and some error because—after all—they were human. The challenge to this position is the lack of common criteria by which to determine truth from error. Each individual is left to affirm or reject the various teachings according to criteria for truth and falsity established by their respective traditions.[4]

A fourth approach regards the foundational religious figures as representatives of radically different visions of reality. According to this view, reality itself is ultimately plural and not singular, many and not only one. There may be many different paths leading to many different peaks.[5] This view validates the teachings of all and avoids any ultimate conflict between them—but its truth or falsity lies beyond verifiability.

My approach follows the lead of B. S. Yadav, whose method may be called scriptural realism.[6] It is a democratization of interreligious dialogue. Scriptural realism extends the golden rule to respect the sacred sources of other religious traditions as you would want them to respect yours. It takes all sacred scriptures seriously as valid means through which wisdom raises her voice. Wisdom, if not censored or suppressed, speaks in and through all scriptures to various people in diverse ways.

Scriptural realism regards sacred texts as mother cows, and the interpreters as calves who jealously contend with each other for access to the pure milk of the word, each claiming to have received better milk than the others. However, the mother cow is untethered and walks from one age to another without depleting or yielding all of her milk to any individual, school or generation of interpreters.

Each sacred scriptural tradition presents its own version of truth. For Mahāvīra, there is no truth above the infinite, eternal, omniscient self. For Buddha everything is momentary; whatever exists changes and whatever doesn't change doesn't exist; truth is *nibbāna*, the unborn and unproduced that is beyond all words and imaginations. Confucius located the source of truth in Heaven and traced its root to the human heart. Laozi situated truth in the *Dao* as the natural way of the universe. For both Muhammad and Moses, God alone is the source and standard of truth, while Kṛṣṇa and Jesus claimed to personally embody transcendent truth itself.

Sacred scriptures speak a wisdom which is hermeneutically hard to hear. There is an interpretive gap between what a text says and what its readers understand. Text-historical scholars seek to bridge the gap by considering the socio-political contexts in which their original audiences would have heard the text. Truth speaks for itself but even truth needs translators and interpreters. Prakrit, Pali, Sanskrit, Chinese, Hebrew, Arabic and Greek are the scriptural languages through which wisdom purports to speak. Sacred scriptures speak a texture of truth in diverse literary devices which transform legends and myths into religious faiths and historical facts. All languages are limited in their capacity to convey truth, which is constrained to speak in and through contradictions. In the pages that follow, wisdom raises her voice from within a cacophony of conflicting claims and counter-claims, each clamoring and contending for its own vision and version of truth.

Notes

1. Proverbs 1:20, *Holy Bible: New International Version*, Zondervan Publishers, 1984.
2. Zacharias, Ravi, *Jesus Among Other Gods*, Thomas Nelson, 2009.
3. Hick, John, *God Has Many Names*, The Westminster Press, 1982.
4. For various Christian approaches to world religions, see Knitter, Paul F., *No Other Name? A Critical Survey of Christian Attitudes Toward the World Religions*, Orbis Books, 1985.
5. Kaplan, Stephen, *Different Paths, Different Summits: A Model for Religious Pluralism*, Rowman and Littlefield Publishers, 2002.
6. Yadav, Bibhuti, "Vaishnavism on Hans Kung: A Hindu Theology of Religious Pluralism" in *Christianity through Non-Christian Eyes*, by Paul J. Griffiths, Faith Meets Faith Series, Orbis Books, 1990.

· 1 ·

MAHĀVĪRA

Introduction

Mahāvīra, which means great hero, is central to the historic foundations of Jainism, among the world's oldest religions. Although its origins are obscured in prehistoric India, today its influence extends throughout the entire earth. Its ancient beginnings are shrouded in the legendary legacy of a long lineage of spiritual conquerors called *jinas* (hence Jainism), who allegedly achieved perfection. And while tradition identifies 24 such conquerors also known as *tīrthaṅkaras*, which means ford-makers or bridge-builders, the only historically verifiable personalities among them are a sixth century BCE Indian ascetic called Mahāvīra and his eighth century BCE predecessor, Pārśva.

Socio-political Context

Sixth century BCE India consisted of rival independent kingdoms, subordinate states and tribes who entered into political and economic alliances. It was a period of relative political peace and prosperity characterized by diverse religious traditions vying with each other for political patronage and public support.

By Mahāvīra's day four distinct social divisions were widely recognized throughout India and religiously legitimated in the *Veda*, the authoritative sacred Sanskrit scriptures of the priestly class. The *Veda* reveals fire sacrifices to fulfill human needs and divulges detailed directions for how priests are to perform them. Access to *Vedic* rituals was limited to the first three social classes: priests (*brahmins*), protectors (*kṣatriyas*), including soldiers, kings and administrators, and producers (*vaiśyas*), including farmers and merchants, all referred to as twice-born because they were eligible to undergo a ritual initiation regarded as a spiritual rebirth into formal *Vedic* study. The fourth social division was servants (*śūdras*), menial laborers who were regarded as morally and spiritually unqualified to access the *Veda* or its rituals.

Vedic culture provided the dominant paradigm which shaped ancient Indian socio-political economy into a matrix of four aims and four stages of life: fulfillment of social responsibility (*dharma*), pursuit of pleasure (*kama*), financial success (*artha*), and liberation (*mokṣa*) are the four aims which are coordinated with four stages: student, householder, forest dweller and homeless wanderer. The first two stages are for the pursuit of the first three aims; the vast majority of people throughout the history of India have been content to pursue these aims without renouncing the world to enter an optional voluntary third stage: living in forest retreats in pursuit of the final aim of life, i.e., liberation from the cyclical syndrome of birth and death. The fourth stage is for those who have attained liberation with nothing left to do or pursue but to wander free as a bird until their body naturally dies and the soul is separated in eternal bliss. The *Vedic* tradition sanctioned renunciation from the world and retirement into the forest only for those who had been previously initiated into *Vedic* study; the final stage of liberation was reserved exclusively for members of the priestly class.

Historically parallel—if not prior—to *Vedic* tradition is an alternative religious culture of people from all divisions of society who renounced the world to live the homeless life of a beggar, practicing meditation and austerities in pursuit of liberation from the recurring cycle of birth and death. Distinctly diverse groups of ascetics represented wide ranging and rival views of reality. They practiced austere ascetic disciplines in order to generate *tapas*—internal spiritual heat which incinerates impurities and prevents any further accumulation. An ascetic is called a *tapasvin*, a generator of spiritual heat.

Mahāvīra championed one such ancient ascetic tradition which flatly rejected *Vedic* revelation and religion, including its sacrificial fire rituals. "He who lights a fire, kills living beings, he who extinguishes it, kills the fire. Therefore a wise man does not light a fire."[1]

Texts as Context

The legacy of Mahāvīra's life and teaching is preserved in the *Jain Sūtras*, composed and compiled over the course of a millennium until committed to writing at a fifth century CE council convened to preserve the oral tradition and protect it from alteration. The texts were orally transmitted by monks in various vernacular languages and eventually written in Prakrit, one of a variety of dialects derived from Sanskrit. In ancient India, business contracts and legal documents were committed to writing but more important bodies of practical or sacred knowledge were methodically memorized and regularly recited because people had more confidence in memory than in manuscripts.

The *Ācārāṅga Sūtra* prescribes correct conduct, plots a pilgrim's progress in pursuit of perfection, and praises the ascetic suffering of Mahāvīra as the inspirational example to emulate. The *Sūtrakṛtāṅga* prepares young monks to defend themselves against rival religious teachers, including Buddhists, confirms them in correct faith, and leads them to the highest goal. It includes discourses that detail the monastic way of life. The stated purpose of the *Uttarādhyayana* is to instruct young monks in their duties, inspire ascetic practice, and warn about hinderances to the homeless life. It features legends of various members from different strata of society who renounced the world to become Jain monks. The *Kalpa Sūtra* is an anthology of biographies featuring some of the 24 conquering heroes, especially Mahāvīra. These are the *Jain Sūtras* in which we encounter Mahāvīra and his message.

Birth and Youth

In the sixth-century before Christ, Mahāvīra was born at Kundagrama, a suburban rest station for travelers near Vaiśālī, the capitol of the Kingdom of Videha in North India. His family possessed both material wealth and political privilege. His father, Raja Siddhartha, was a ruling elder of one of the several regional republican aristocracies. His mother, Triśala, was the sister of King Ketaka of Vaiśālī to whom Siddhartha's republic was allied and subordinate. Through his mother, Mahāvīra was also related to King Bimbisāra of Magadha who was married to the daughter of King Ketaka.

Mahāvīra's parents were devout lay followers of Parśva, the predecessor of Mahāvīra in the long line of spiritual conquerors.[2] They named him Vardhamāna, which means increasing, because astrologers had prophesied that he would bring increased political prestige and social success to his family.[3] Accordingly, from the day of his conception forward, the prosperity and popularity of his parents continued to abound.[4]

Textual tradition records that he was married by arrangement to a young wife, Yaśodā, with whom he fathered a daughter, Anogga, and he experienced the pleasures and pressures of family life. Little else is known about his early years because Jain biographers focus almost exclusively on details of Mahāvīra's spiritual life and regard other information as totally irrelevant. Inclined toward spiritual aspirations from an early age, he repeatedly sought parental permission to renounce the world of social roles, relationships and responsibilities to search for enlightenment, but his parents' preferences prevailed and the respectful Mahāvīra remained at home.

Renunciation and Wanderings

At age 28, after his parents died, Mahāvīra again expressed resolve to renounce the world but, in deference to his elder brother's wishes, and so as not to compound the extended family's grief, he stayed at home for another two years.[5] Each day throughout the final year at home, he gradually gave away all his possessions to the poor.[6] By age thirty, having given away everything, including his clothing, he renounced the world and walked naked in pursuit of purification.

> Mahāvīra was ceremoniously paraded with great pomp, carried by an entourage to the outskirts of his hometown to the foot of a tree, where he descended from his palanquin, removed his jewelry, garlands, fine clothing, and, after two and one-half days, without drinking water or eating food, all alone, with no one else present, with his bare hand tore out his hair in five clumps and became homeless.[7]

Whereas *Vedic* renunciation of the world was open only to elderly people who had already fulfilled their pursuit of pleasure, wealth, and social responsibility, including the production of a grandson, Mahāvīra saw no point in waiting for old age.

Sometime soon after his formal ritual renunciation of the world, Mahāvīra joined a company of Jain monks, followers of Pārśva, who took four vows including non-violence, truthfulness, non-stealing, and non-possession. Mahāvīra's radical extension of non-violence to include compassion for all living beings soon became problematic within Pārśva's monastic community. Tradition recalls how cows, driven by hunger from drought, wandered into the monastery grounds and began eating the straw huts in which the monks lived. Whereas the other monks chased the cows away with sticks, Mahāvīra permitted them to literally eat him out of house and home, then parted company with the community of Pārśva and set out on a 12-year trek throughout Northeast India.

Jain sacred texts carefully chronicle the itinerary of places, people, and perils Mahāvīra encountered during his dozen years meandering as a naked mendicant. Because he walked nude, never bathed, refused to respond to greetings, and begged food with his unwashed hands, people found him shocking, disgusting, repulsive, and repugnant.[8] He was ridiculed, maligned, taunted, insulted, tormented, tortured, beaten, cut, attacked by dogs, and imprisoned on false charges.[9] Nevertheless, he endured the abuses with equanimity and indifference because he lived above likes and dislikes, regarding pleasure and pain as totally the same.[10]

Way of Life

Mahāvīra likened a monk's life to a heroic warrior who goes forth bravely into battle without looking back or fearing death.

> A monk who exerts himself in a similar way, should slip off the ties that bind him to his house. Putting aside all undertakings, he should wander about for the liberation of his soul.[11] Leaving his wealth, family, friends and property, leaving sorrow that never ceases, a monk should wander about without any worldly interests.[12]

Spiritual warfare is Mahāvīra's way:

> Fight with yourself. Why fight external foes? He who conquers self through the self will obtain happiness. The five senses, anger, pride, delusion and greed—difficult to conquer is one's self; but when that is conquered, everything is conquered.[13]

Mahāvīra resolved to follow a fivefold discipline of never staying in the house of an unfriendly person, standing statue-still, staying silent, eating only from his hand, and refraining from politeness to householders. He spent endless hours in silence, standing motionless in meditation even in the midst of crowds. He never spoke unless spoken to but even then, whenever people addressed him, he often walked away silently.[14] His naked, unwashed body and unkempt hair were habitation for insects, whose bites inflicted bloody wounds that Mahāvīra bore with the indifference and equanimity of an accomplished ascetic. Later he would instruct his followers:

> Suffering from insects a great sage remains undisturbed. Like an elephant at the head of the battle kills the enemy, so does a hero in self-control conquer the internal enemy. He should not scare away any insects, nor keep them off, nor be provoked to passion by them. Tolerate living beings, do not kill them though they eat your flesh and blood.[15]

He practiced prolonged, uninterrupted meditation and severe austerities. In the summer he meditated in the hot sun and walked through sunbaked fields, and in winter he meditated naked in the open air.[16] As he walked carefully, he kept his eyes fixed on the ground so as not to injure or crush any insects. He slept in abandoned buildings, cremation grounds, gardens and other solitary places.[17] The meager amount of food he consumed came from begging. However, whenever he saw any other person, animal or bird waiting for food at a home, he would quietly move on.[18] He fasted sometimes for days, weeks or months at a time.[19]

Enlightenment and Ministry

Jain sacred literature describes in detail how Mahāvīra achieved enlightenment at age 42 after 12 years of arduous ascetic practice.

> On the bank of a river, in the field of a householder, under a tree, in a squatting position with heels joined, exposing himself to the hot sun, with knees high and head bowed low, in deep abstract meditation, he reached the complete and full, unobstructed, unimpeded, infinite and supreme knowledge and intuition.[20]

After attaining enlightenment, Mahāvīra addressed a small assembly:

> I am all knowing, all seeing, and possess infinite knowledge. Whether I am walking or standing still, whether I sleep or remain awake, the supreme knowledge and intuition are constantly and continuously present with me.[21]

The source of Mahāvīra's happiness is not to be found in the fulfillment of social responsibility, financial success, or sensual pleasure but dwells deep inside himself. It is indescribable joy, undetectable to onlookers, mystically experienced in the soul but far beyond the reach of the senses and the mind.[22]

For the next 30 years, Mahāvīra traversed Northeast India as an itinerant monk, teaching the path of purification and attracting disciples from all walks of life. His discourses and discussions convinced and converted politicians, paupers, priests, and all kinds of people. Eventually the many monastic followers of Pārśva recognized Mahāvīra as the spiritual successor and became his disciples.[23]

He passed the four-month rainy season each year in sheltered monastic retreats with communities that he himself established and regulated throughout three decades of ministry. Mahāvīra was a genius organizer and administrator. He arranged his disciples into four distinct divisions—male and female monastics, and male and female laity—prescribing particular directions and disciplines appropriate to each group.

By providing a path toward perfection even for laity, including women, and by involving families in the support of the monastic mission, Mahāvīra managed to integrate Jainism into the socio-economic fabric of Indian culture. Lay followers could plod the path toward purification and perfection though not with the same prospect for success as the monastics whom they maintained with material support.

Death and Legacy

At age 72, aware that death was imminent, Mahāvīra selected a secluded spot under a tree, inspected the ground, carefully relocated all living beings, sat down and resolved to face death with a fast. After uninterrupted, silent, seated meditation, he exited his body and entered the boundless beatitude of pure being, awareness and bliss.[24]

The final aim of the spiritual life is the soul's realization of its inherent perfections. Ultimately the soul cannot experience its absolute perfections until after death. For this reason, the final stage of the purification process is a voluntary fast unto death.[25] The body is the last bondage from which only death can set the soul free. It is the final and most difficult attachment to overcome.

Through the noble death fast, Mahāvīra faced the mortality and finality of human life, not as an involuntary victim, but as a courageous conqueror, aggressively pursuing purification and perfection. The logic of the fast unto death follows from Mahāvīra's belief that eating entails killing because living beings must die to feed others. Life is sustained by death. This is the milieu of misery pervading Mahāvīra's critique of life in the world. "All beings want happiness and hate pain; therefore this is the essence of wisdom: not to injure or kill anything."[26]

Teachings

Soul and Matter

God is entirely irrelevant to Mahāvīra's pathway to purification and perfection.[27] While denying a creator God and denouncing dependence on any divine grace or supernatural assistance, Mahāvīra contended that the universe is composed of two broad categories of reality—living and nonliving—soul and matter.[28]

Soul. The word for soul (jīva) is the same as the word for life because Mahāvīra believed that all forms of life embody a soul. Soul is a subtle spiritual substance without beginning or end. It is not created and cannot be destroyed. Each soul is inherently characterized by unobstructed knowledge, unbounded energy and uninterrupted bliss.

According to Mahāvīra, there are innumerable souls inhabiting the infinitely diverse material universe. Living souls are of two kinds: those still caught up in saṃsāra—the turbulent stream of birth and death—and those who have been purified, perfected and liberated from it. Souls who are still recycling through saṃsāra are of two kinds: movable and immovable. Earth-bodies, water-bodies and plants are immovable whereas fire-bodies, wind-bodies and organic bodies, including animals and humans, are movable.

Embodied souls are further classified according to the number of sense organs they possess.[29] All forms of life, including earth, water, wind, fire, and plants, possess the sense of touch. Injuring or killing living beings, even to eat, incurs karmic consequence; the greater the number of sense organs possessed by that which is eaten, the denser the karmic cloud that clings to the soul who eats it.

Though a monk's body be weakened by hunger, a monk who is strong in self-control and ascetic practice should not cut or cause another to cut anything to be eaten, nor cook it or cause another to cook it.[30]

Mahāvīra and his followers begged only for left-over food that was not prepared purposely for them. "A true monk should not accept food and drink that has been especially prepared for him involving the slaughter of living beings."[31]

Matter. By contrast, matter is material substance comprised of atomic particles that float freely through time and space. The word for matter is a compound (*pudgala*) combining opposite ideas into a single concept; it means that which comes together and that which falls apart. Souls are embodied in matter, which obscures their inherent omniscience, limits their infinite energy, and inhibits their intrinsic joy. Mahāvīra taught that people are in bondage, encased in a subtle substance that is attracted to the soul by thought, speech and action.

Karma and Reincarnation

Karma. Matter and soul are all that is; there is no other category of reality. *Karma* is matter. This is a unique and peculiar Jain understanding. Other Indian philosophers regarded *karma* as a transcendent ethical principle or psychological force but Mahāvīra considered *karma* to be material substances that are attracted to the soul through bodily actions, thoughts and speech. Like dust covering a lamp prevents light from illuminating objects, *karma* prevents the soul from realizing and experiencing its own infinite knowledge, unlimited energy and boundless bliss.

The soul is not heir to an original sin but to a primordial bondage encased in *karma*. There is no first cause of the soul's attachment to *karmic* matter. The soul's association with *karma* is without any origin. Innumerable souls have been forever recycling from body to body through the perpetual process of birth and death; bondage to *karma* is the existential starting point from which the soul might finally find release.

All *karma* is not equal but varies in terms of duration, intensity and effect.[32] Mahāvīra delineated different categories of *karma*, not all of which are defiling to the soul. Defiling *karma* is the subtle substance that sticks to the soul, stunting and stymieing its spiritual progress toward purification and perfection. Defiling *karma* hinders the ability of the soul to know itself, and prevents the soul from recognizing its true identity; it also deludes people into mistaking the activities of the body, mind and senses for the soul itself.

Other kinds of *karma*, though not defiling, nevertheless perpetuate attachment to the body and its senses. Even good *karma* is only relatively good, though ultimately bad since all actions, good and bad, produce consequences that must be experienced sooner or later, either in this life or another embodiment. Some *karma* is better than others, but all kinds of *karma* must eventually be eliminated and avoided to liberate the soul from bondage. "Therefore a wise one should know the different kinds of *karma* and should make every effort to destroy them."[33]

> One should know what causes the bondage of soul and knowing it one should remove it. What causes the bondage of the soul according to Mahāvīra and what must one know in order to remove it? He who owns even a small property in living or lifeless things or consents to others holding it, will not be delivered from misery.[34]

Renunciation of possessions, violence, friends and family is essential, not optional, for liberation from the otherwise endless rounds of birth and death.

> If a person kills living beings or causes others to kill them or consents to their killing them, his iniquity will go on increasing. A person who makes the interests of his family and friends his own, will suffer much; for the number of those whose interest he takes to heart constantly increases. All one's wealth and nearest relatives cannot protect him from future misery; knowing this, one will get rid of *karma*.[35]

Reincarnation. Each individual soul undergoes innumerable embodiments from single sense organisms to more complex creatures who possess two to five sense organs until the natural re-incarnation process culminates in a human being.[36]

> Living beings who are born again and again in ever-recurring births bewildered through the influence of their actions, distressed and suffering, undergo misery in non-human births. By the cessation of *karma*, living beings will be born as humans.[37]

Only in a human body can a soul strive to achieve liberation from bondage. "This human body is not easy to attain."[38] "A rare chance, in the long course of time, is human birth for a living being; hard are the consequences of action."[39]

Like gold encased in rock, the soul is surrounded by the suppressing weight of *karma*. Every being wants to be happy but goes unfulfilled for failure to recognize the true nature of the soul. Mahāvīra identified four things which are very difficult for a living being to obtain: human birth, instruction in the path of perfection, belief in it, and the energy to practice it.[40]

The Path

"What is the path Mahāvīra taught by which a person can cross the stream of birth and death? Tell us how we should describe that path if someone were to ask us about it."[41] "Mastering the senses and avoiding wrong, one should do no harm to anybody, neither by thoughts, words nor actions."[42] "Indifferent to worldly objects, one should wander about treating all creatures in the world as one wants to be treated."[43]

By what acts can one escape the cycle of birth and death? Mahāvīra cultivated the art of inaction. "He who does not undertake new acts, does not acquire *karma*."[44] "By renouncing activity one acquires no new *karma* and destroys that which was previously accumulated."[45] It took Mahāvīra 12 years to achieve the status of conqueror over *karmic* bondage, and accordingly he prescribed an arduous process for the pursuit of purification and perfection.[46] The path is marked by the three jewels of Jainism: faith, knowledge and conduct.[47]

Faith. Mahāvīra's pathway to purification begins when the soul, in a spontaneous fleeting flash of profound spiritual insight, briefly experiences its own infinite knowledge, energy and bliss. This is the birth of faith which is trust in the soul itself as the ultimate source of an eternal life of infinite knowledge, energy and bliss.

Knowledge. Knowledge is the experience of the soul itself, not in relation to God, but a direct, mystical awareness in which the soul knows itself alone, isolated from the conditions and consequences of *karma*. However, this initial vision that generates faith and knowledge is easily forgotten and overwhelmed by the crushing weight of *karmic* consequences resulting from habits of daily life in the world. Nevertheless, Mahāvīra taught that this initial faith and profound personal insight into the soul provides the assurance and ambition required to pursue and achieve freedom from bondage.

Conduct. All further progress along the path is predicated upon performance of correct conduct embodied in the five vows of virtuous behavior, four of which were inherited from the previous Jain tradition of Pārśva: non-violence, truthfulness, non-stealing, non-possession, and a fifth added by Mahāvīra, namely celibacy for monks and sexual fidelity for laity.[48]

Foremost among Jain virtues and values is non-violence.[49] It is the foun-
tain of virtue from which all the others flow. Violence in its various forms—
mental, verbal and physical—causes *karma* to cling to the soul.[50] Doing violence to other beings attracts the most detrimental kinds of *karmic* substance.
Mahāvīra called for a radical and universal application of non-violence, prescribing conscientious compassion and empathetic concern toward the earth's
entire environment, including the global community of all living beings.[51]

He prescribed a comprehensive code of conduct, including walking carefully not to maim or kill any living beings, speaking sparingly and sensitively,
begging for permitted food not purposely prepared for the monk, receiving
and inspecting instruments necessary for the life of a monk (a broom to sweep
away insects from the path, a begging bowl, and a cloth to place in front of
their mouths while speaking so as not to inadvertently swallow insects, and
for straining living organisms from water so as not to carelessly kill them),
relieving themselves of bodily waste in appropriate places without injury to
living beings, preventing the mind from wandering into sexual fantasy by contemplation and study, preventing the tongue from improper speech by temporary, periodic vows of silence, and placing and maintaining the body in an
immovable posture.

Summary

Each soul is totally responsible for its own ignorance and enlightenment, its
own bondage and liberation. Mahāvīra places the onus for the soul's corrupt
condition squarely on the shoulders of each individual. "My own self is the
doer and un-doer of misery and happiness; my own self is my friend or enemy
according to whether I act well or badly."[52] "All living beings owe their present form of existence to their own *karma*."[53] "A monk should silently repeat
to himself: A man must come and go according to his *karma* alone without
deriving any help from others."[54]

The pathway to purification is extremely difficult. It is a long, arduous
process of perpetual practice in ascetic disciplines and self-denying behaviors
designed to eliminate previously accrued *karma* and prevent its additional,
future influx and accumulation. There were many other ancient ascetic religious leaders but none more severe or austere than Mahāvīra. Whereas rival
renunciation groups also engaged in a variety of painful practices, Mahāvīra
elevated asceticism to a supreme spiritual status, declaring it to be the high-
way to enlightenment, liberation and release.

Between Mahāvīra and Jesus

Between Renunciation and Repentance

Mahāvīra voluntarily gave away all his possessions to the poor before willingly renouncing all worldly ambition in search of salvation. His renunciation of all possessions resonates with the response Jesus gave to the rich young ruler who asked what he must do to inherit the kingdom of God. "This one thing you lack, give away all your possessions to the poor and come follow me."[55] The privileged prince went away sad because he was too attached to his wealth. He did not possess his wealth as much as it possessed him. Jesus, like Mahāvīra, was an ascetic who called his disciples to emulate his simple, self-restrained, humble way of life. Jesus asks: "What does it proffer a person to gain the world but lose their soul?"[56] Mahāvīra called people to renunciation of the world while Jesus called people to repentance from sin.

Mahāvīra and Jesus were both pedestrian, itinerant mendicants who depended on the hospitality of householders for their food and fiscal support. Mahāvīra often slept in forests and jungles, under trees, in cremation grounds, abandoned buildings and other isolated places. Mahāvīra, like Jesus, had no place of his own to call home. Jesus said: "Foxes have holes, birds have nests, but the Son of Man has no place to lay his head."[57]

Mahāvīra, like Jesus, directed his disciples to wander without possessions, begging and eating with their bare, unwashed hands. Mahāvīra never stayed in any village more than a single night nor remained in any city more than five days because he did not want to become attached or too comfortable. "Different from other people, a monk should wander about, he should acquire no property; but not being attached to householders, he should live without a fixed residence."[58] In contrast, Jesus counseled his disciples to stay in one home as long as they remained in any particular place, whether town or country. He directed them to develop disciples by cultivating personal relationships.[59]

Mahāvīra and Jesus held different perspectives on the purpose of life. Mahāvīra eschewed social contact in search of a solitary salvation but Jesus promoted personal relationships for the purpose of building the kingdom of God. Mahāvīra discouraged his followers from courting the favor or friendship of householders, and dissuaded them from providing child-care, counseling or healing services; he did not want his disciples to engage in economic exchange or become dependent on anyone in particular. Jesus directed his disciples to declare and demonstrate the arrival of the kingdom of God by healing the sick, casting out demons, and demonstrating love for each other. Jesus did not promote a path to self-enlightenment, rather he preached the way of repentance, forgiveness and freedom from sin.

Between Karma and Sin

Mahāvīra claimed to have conquered *karma* for himself alone. The word *karma* comes from a verbal root which means to act and to produce; hence *karma* refers to actions and the results they produce. Everyone must suffer the consequences of their own actions. Even if someone wished to suffer vicariously on behalf of family or friends, Mahāvīra's doctrine of *karma* precludes the possibility.

> One person cannot take upon himself the pains of another; one man cannot experience what another has done. Individually a person is born, and individually a person dies; the bonds of relationship are not able to save one.[60]

Jesus came to conquer sin—not *karma*. Sin is disobedience to God which incurs a debt and a stain that must be remitted and removed.[61] Jesus claimed to have conquered sin, not for himself but on behalf of sinners. Jesus referred to sin as a master to whom people have become enslaved: "Very truly I tell you, everyone who sins is a slave to sin. If you hold my teachings, you are really my disciples. Then you will know the truth and the truth will set you free."[62] Jesus saw himself as the savior sent by God to free sinners from slavery to sin: "For the Son of Man came not to be served but to serve and to give his life as a ransom for many."[63]

What Christians Might Learn From Mahāvīra

Nonviolence

Mahāvīra magnifies the golden rule and extends compassion to every living being.[64] By cultivating care for all beings as co-heirs of the grace of life, Christians can condition their conscience with concern for the entire living environment. Those who practice nonviolence to all forms of life are far more likely to treat people of different races, religions and ethnicities with empathy. Moreover, Mahāvīra's virtue of non-violence and non-injury to the entire

eco-system may well be humanity's last hope to save the planet from the imminent and irreversible effects of global warming.

Notes

1. *Sūtrakṛtāṅga* 1:7:6, Jacobi, Hermann, *Jain Sūtra*, Sacred Books of the East, Volume XVL, Delhi: Motilal Banarsidass, 1964. All references to the *Sūtrakṛtāṅga* are based on this translation unless otherwise noted.
2. *Ācārāṅga Sūtra* 2:15:16, Jacobi, Hermann, *Jain Sūtra*, Sacred Books of the East, Volume XVL, Delhi: Motilal Banarsidass, 1964. All references to the *Ācārāṅga Sūtra* are based on this translation unless otherwise noted.
3. *Ācārāṅga Sūtra*; 2:15:12; *Kalpa Sūtra* 4:64–65; 4:90–91; 5:106–107.
4. *Kalpa Sūtra* 4:90–91, Jacobi, Hermann, *Jain Sūtra*, Sacred Books of the East, Volume XVL, Delhi : Motilal Banarsidass, 1964. All references to the *Kalpa Sūtra* are based on this trans-lation unless otherwise noted.
5. *Kalpa Sūtra* 5:110.
6. *Kalpa Sūtra* 5:112.
7. *Ācārāṅga Sūtra* 2:15:23.
8. *Uttarādhyayana Sūtra* 2:36–37, Jacobi, Hermann, *Jain Sūtra*, Sacred Books of the East, Volume XVL, Delhi: Motilal Banarsidass, 1964. All references to *Uttarādhyayana Sūtra* are based on this translation unless otherwise noted.
9. *Ācārāṅga Sūtra* 1:3:1.
10. *Uttarādhyayana Sūtra* 2:24; 14:32.
11. *Sūtrakṛtāṅga* 1:3:6–7.
12. *Sūtrakṛtāṅga* 1:9:7.
13. *Uttarādhyayana Sūtra* 9:35–36.
14. *Ācārāṅga Sūtra* 1:8:1:6.
15. *Uttarādhyayana Sūtra* 2:10–11.
16. *Ācārāṅga Sūtra* 1:8:4:3–4.
17. *Ācārāṅga Sūtra* 1:8:2:2–3.
18. *Ācārāṅga Sūtra* 1:8:4:10–12.
19. *Ācārāṅga Sūtra* 1:8:4:7–9.
20. *Kalpa Sūtra* 5:120.
21. *Ācārāṅga Sūtra*: 2:15:26.
22. *Uttarādhyayana Sūtra* 14:19.
23. *Uttarādhyayana Sūtra* 23.
24. *Kalpa Sūtra* 5:149.
25. *Ācārāṅga Sūtra* 1:6.
26. *Sūtrakṛtāṅga* 1:11:9.
27. *Sūtrakṛtāṅga* 1:1:3:5–9.
28. Matter includes time, space, motion and rest.
29. *Uttarādhyayana Sūtra* 36.
30. *Uttarādhyayana Sūtra*: 2:1.

31. *Sūtrakṛtāṅga* 1:11:14.
32. *Uttarādhyayana Sūtra* 33:1–15.
33. *Uttarādhyayana Sūtra* 33:25.
34. *Sūtrakṛtāṅga* 1:1:1–2.
35. *Sūtrakṛtāṅga* 1:1:3–5.
36. *Uttarādhyayana Sūtra* 3:2–7; 10.
37. *Uttarādhyayana Sūtra* 3:6–7.
38. *Sūtrakṛtāṅga* 1:15:17.
39. *Uttarādhyayana Sūtra* 10:4.
40. *Uttarādhyayana Sūtra* 3:1.
41. *Sūtrakṛtāṅga* 1:11:1–3.
42. *Sūtrakṛtāṅga* 1:1:12.
43. *Sūtrakṛtāṅga* 1:1:33.
44. *Sūtrakṛtāṅga* 1:15:7.
45. *Uttarādhyayana Sūtra* 29:37.
46. *Uttarādhyayana Sūtra* 28–31; *Sūtrakṛtāṅga* 1:11.
47. *Uttarādhyayana Sūtra* 23:33; 28:1–3.
48. *Ācārāṅga Sūtra* 2:15; *Uttarādhyayana Sūtra* 21:12.
49. *Ācārāṅga Sūtra* 1:4.
50. *Sūtrakṛtāṅga* 1:11:9–12.
51. *Ācārāṅga Sūtra* 1:1.
52. *Uttarādhyayana Sūtra* 20:37.
53. *Sūtrakṛtāṅga* 1:2:18.
54. *Sūtrakṛtāṅga* 1:13:18.
55. Mark 10:21; Matthew 19:21, *Holy Bible: New International Version*, Zondervan Publishers, 1984. All references to the Bible are based on this translation unless otherwise noted.
56. Mark 8:36; Matthew 16:26.
57. Luke 9:58.
58. *Uttarādhyayana Sūtra* 2:19.
59. Luke 9:4; Mark 6:10.
60. *Sūtrakṛtāṅga* 2:1:40–41.
61. Anderson, G. A., *Sin: A History*, Yale University Press, 2009.
62. John 8:34, 31.
63. Mark 10:45.
64. *Sūtrakṛtāṅga* 1:11:33.

· 2 ·

BUDDHA

Introduction

A global religion, Buddhism has spread to every continent and country from Cambodia to California. Since the second century before Christ, when King Aśoka sent emissaries from India throughout Southeast Asian countries and kingdoms, Buddhist principles and practices continue to characterize the cultures. Buddhism adapted through migration and merger into numerous other alien cultures. Buddhist missionary monks historically and strategically adapted Buddhist beliefs and behaviors to accommodate and effectively appeal to its various host cultures throughout Asia, Australia, Europe and the Americas. Today Buddhism has become many different things to many different people.

This chapter provides neither a general overview of Buddhism, nor a summary of any particular school of its philosophy or practice; rather, it paints a picture of one giant personality, portraying the life and teachings of its historical founder, Siddhattha Gotama of the Śakhya clan—the boy born to become Buddha.

Socio-political Context

Buddha lived during the sixth and fifth centuries before Christ in North Central India and inherited the same socio-political situation as Mahāvīra (see chapter 1). Early Buddhist texts reveal that the region in which he wandered was composed of four independent kingdoms, several subordinate oligarchic republics, and many small tribes that formed alliances with the kings who protected them in exchange for loyalty and tribute. Once a year subordinate rulers would journey to the king's capitol for ritual renewal of their oaths of allegiance. It was a period of political peace and stability during which numerous rival religious sects competed for royal patronage and material support in the form of robes, meals, medicine and monasteries.

The independent ruling republic into which Buddha was born was beholden to the sovereignty of King Pasendai, who ruled the kingdom of Kosala from its capitol in Sāvatthī, where he generously donated a park and monastery for Buddha and his community of monks to live in during the annual rainy seasons. King Bimbisāra ruled Magadha from his capitol at Rājagaha and was also a patron who donated land and built dwellings for Buddha's monastic community called the *sangha*. Buddhist scriptures frequently mention the names of kings, capitols, crossroads, parks and prominent personalities which firmly situate Buddha on historical ground.

Texts as Context

Sources for the life and teachings of Buddha are preserved in Pali, which Buddha would have known because it was the official language for the administration of government and courts of law. It was a transregional language spoken only by the educated but easily understood by all.

As soon as Buddha died, his leading disciples began asking each other what they might do to ensure the preservation of his words. Three months after the Buddha's death, a senior monk summoned an assembly of 500 monks and addressed them: "Let us recite the Buddha's teachings and rules together so that no wrong doctrines or rules creep in."[1]

Throughout a seven-month period, the presiding senior monk questioned two distinguished disciples of the Buddha, one renowned for his knowledge of Buddha's discourses and the other for his expertise in the monastic code of conduct. The expert in remembering the discourses was

Ānanda, a cousin of Buddha and his personal servant during the last 24 years of his life. The expert in remembering the monastic code was Upāli, formerly a barber who had renounced the world together with his friend Ānanda and others.

The presiding monk alternately posed questions to the two esteemed experts who answered by reciting the relevant words of Buddha. Ānanda provided the historical situation and setting in which each discourse was delivered and began each recitation with the words "Thus have I heard" indicating that he was an ear witness of Buddha's utterances. Upāli presented the incident and circumstance that motivated Buddha to institute each rule of monastic conduct and began each of his recitations with the words "The occasion was this." The assembly of 500 monks affirmed the accuracy of their answers by remaining silent and spoke out only when they had a question, correction or clarification to contribute.

Having established an authorized canon of Buddha's discourses and monastic rules, the monks meticulously memorized and transmitted them to the younger generation through reliable methods of recitation and repetition. Over the next two centuries, two more conferences to clarify and confirm the canon were convened; these culminated in the development of a third collection of teachings that provide a philosophical analysis of the factors of existence. The didactic discourses, monastic rules, and philosophical treatises were collected into what has come to be called the *tipiṭika*, three baskets. After four centuries of careful oral preservation and transmission, the *tipiṭika* was committed to writing on the island of Sri Lanka, which had become a bastion of Buddhism.

Birth and Youth

Buddha was born into the prominent aristocratic family named Gotama and led a life of political privilege.[2] His father, King Suddhōdanna (he who grows pure rice), possessed parochial power as a ruler of the Śakhyan republic, a rural farming community. Although Siddhattha spent the first 29 years of his life in Kapilvastu, he was not born there. Before his mother was able to complete the journey to her parents' village where she had hoped to deliver her child according to custom, she gave birth while standing and leaning against a tree in the grove of Lumbinī. Māyādevī died one week later but not before witnessing the name-giving ceremony of her son Siddhattha, meaning he who hits his aim. He is frequently referred to in scripture by his family name Gotama and sometimes called Śakyamuni, sage of the Śakhya clan. His mother's younger sister, Mahāpajāpatti, was also married to Suddhōdanna and raised Siddhattha as her step-son along with a daughter named Sundarīnandā and her natural son Nandā, who was born just a few days after Siddhattha.

Three days after Siddhattha's birth, his father summoned astrologers to pronounce promising words concerning his son's future. Pandering to the politician, some fortune tellers predicted the boy would become a universal monarch to unify India's many rival kingdoms, but one elderly dissenting voice forecasted that Siddhattha would renounce the world and become a spiritual giant to illuminate the ignorant.[3] Alarmed and alerted, Siddhattha's father pampered and protected him, prohibiting and preventing him from seeing the suffering plight of ordinary people.

> I was delicate, most delicate, supremely delicate. Lily pools were made for me at my father's house solely for my benefit. My turban, tunic, lower garments and cloak were all made of the finest cloth. A white umbrella was held over me day and night so that no cold or heat or dust or grit or dew might inconvenience me.[4]

To distract him, his father lavishly provided Siddhattha with three different dwellings, one suited to each of the several South Asian seasons. Dancing girls and dazzling diversions dominated the days Siddhattha passed inside his palace walls, which eventually became like a prison to him, blocking his view and blinding his vision of raw reality.[5]

Four Sights

Feeling like a caged elephant raging for release, scripture describes how Siddhattha eventually prevailed upon his father to permit him an open adventure—a chauffeured, chaperoned, guided tour around the village streets to see the sights of everyday life in the world beyond the walls, gardens and gates of his palatial estates. For the first time, the young Siddhattha saw people suffering from disease, decrepitude and death. He also saw a monk with a shaved head, robe, and begging bowl; this alerted him to the option of renouncing the world and later inspired him to do just that.

> Before my enlightenment, being myself subject to birth, aging, ailment, death, sorrow and defilement, I sought after what was also subject to these things. Then I

thought: Since I am subject to these things, why do I seek after things that are also subject to them? What if, seeing danger in such things, I sought after the unborn, un-aging, un-ailing, deathless, sorrow-less, undefiled supreme cessation of bondage, *nibbāna*?[6]

On the occasion of a ploughing ritual to initiate the planting season, the young Siddhattha separated himself and sat secluded under the shade of a tree; there he enjoyed the first stage of meditation and watched as his father ceremoniously ploughed the ground, cutting up worms and killing creatures dwelling in the earth. Siddhattha then concluded that life is miserable, full of disappointment, disease and death.[7]

In an effort to further bind him to the world, Siddhattha's father arranged for him to be married at age 16 to his cousin, the ever-cheerful Yaśodharā; her hand he was required to win from his uncle, King Dandapani, in an archery contest against other eligible princes from the Gotama clan. It seems his uncle was reluctant to give his daughter in marriage to Siddhattha, who already had a reputation for being a pensive pacifist rather than a proud protector prince. For 13 years they remained childless but eventually Yaśodharā bore a son whom they named Rāhula, meaning fetter or chain; his name was fitting because Siddhattha felt parenthood, marriage and household life were a burdensome bondage that was difficult to break.

Before my enlightenment, I thought house life is crowded and dusty. It is not easy, living in a household to lead a holy life as utterly pure and perfect as a polished shell. Suppose I shave off my hair and beard, put on a yellow robe and went forth into homelessness?[8]

Renunciation and Wanderings

At age 29, in the middle of the night while his wife and infant son slept soundly, Siddhattha summoned his servant, mounted his horse, and rode to the edge of his father's domain. There he exchanged his fine clothes for his servant's simple garb and cut off his beard and hair. With that cut, Siddhattha renounced the world of social roles, relationships, and responsibilities, and began a six-year search for enlightenment.

While still a black-haired man in the prime of life, I shaved off my hair and beard— though my parents wished otherwise and grieved with tearful faces—and I put on the yellow robe and went forth from the house into homelessness.[9]

Not one to wander aimlessly, Siddhattha sought instruction from spiritual sages, teachers renowned for their wisdom and knowledge.[10] He wandered to beg for food toward Rājagaha, the capital of the kingdom of Magadha, and then found a cave for shelter in the hills surrounding the city. The first sage he encountered was Āḷāra Kālāma, who welcomed Siddhattha as his student and trained him in meditation. By direct meditative insight, Siddhattha quickly fathomed Kālāma's philosophy and experienced the meditational base of nothingness. Although his teacher elevated him to equal standing and commissioned him as a co-teacher, Siddhattha thought to himself:

> This teaching does not lead to dispassion, to fading out of lust, to cessation, to peace, to direct full knowledge, to enlightenment, but only to the base consisting of nothingness. I was not satisfied with that teaching. I left it to pursue my search and found Uddaka Rāmaputta.[11]

From Uddaka Rāmaputta, Siddhattha learned quickly to experience a higher meditative state consisting of neither perception nor non-perception, but again he concluded that it did not lead to enlightenment. Finding neither of the sages' methods or messages fully satisfactory, Siddhattha set out all alone, forging his own path to end pain and terminate suffering.

Eventually, Siddhattha joined company with a group of five wandering ascetics who practiced extreme austerities just as severe as the methods of Mahāvīra. Siddhattha described in detail some of the practices:

> With my teeth clinched and my tongue pressed against the roof of my mouth, I beat down, restrained and crushed my mind with my mind. Sweat ran from my armpits while I did so. Though tireless energy was generated in me and unremitting mindfulness established, yet my body was overwhelmed and uncalm because I was exhausted by the painful effort but such painful feelings gained no power over my mind.[12]

He further describes practicing a form of meditation without breathing, but it too ended in exhaustion. Next, he decided to radically reduce his daily diet to one bean, one grain of rice and a single sesame seed.

> My body reached a state of extreme emaciation. My spine looked like a string of beads. If I touched my belly skin, I encountered my backbone too because my belly skin cleaved to my backbone. If I tried to ease my body by rubbing my limbs with my hands, the hair, rotted at its roots, fell away from my body as I rubbed because of eating so little.[13]

Siddhattha reflected on his painful ascetic practices and concluded that he had achieved no distinction higher than human nature and asked himself if there might be another way to enlightenment. He remembered the pleasure he experienced in secluded meditation under the tree during his father's ritual ploughing ceremony and reckoned that meditation was the way to the enlightenment that he sought. He thought to himself:

> Why am I afraid of such pleasure? It is pleasure that has nothing to do with sensual desires and unwholesome things but it is not possible to attain that pleasure with a body so extensively emaciated so I ate some solid food, boiled rice and bread.[14]

When his five ascetic companions saw him eating rice and bread, they became disgusted and left him, thinking that he had become self-indulgent and given up the struggle for enlightenment to return to a life of luxury.

Siddhattha abandoned extreme austerities, denouncing them as futile and worthless. He parted company with his five ascetic companions and pursued the solution to suffering, traveling all by himself, alone. After sufficient solitude and wandering, sensing the dawn of enlightenment, Siddhattha sought a single tree and sat down beneath it. Placing one hand on the ground and pointing the other upward, calling earth and sky to bear witness, he vowed never to move from that spot unless and until he became fully enlightened.

Enlightenment and Ministry

After long hours of meditation in which Siddhattha overcame all influences and temptations to abandon his quest, his enlightenment continued dawning in three distinct stages.[15] First, he attained insight into the details of his own innumerable past lives. In the second stage, he gained insight into the universal process of birth, death, and reincarnation, understanding how beings pass on according to their actions. The final stage of Siddhattha's enlightenment consisted in grasping the Four Noble Truths: suffering, its origin, its cessation and the way leading to its cessation.

For one full week he sat beneath the tree experiencing the bliss of deliverance and musing on the meaning of his enlightenment. For the next month Siddhattha wandered from place to place enjoying the bliss of enlightenment, meditating beneath the shade of trees. While sitting in one place for a week, two wealthy merchants encountered him, listened to his teaching called the *dhamma*, and became his first followers.

During another week of meditation in a different village, Siddhattha began to doubt that anyone would be able to understand or practice the *dhamma,* which was so difficult to discover especially for people attracted and attached to sensual pleasures. Eventually he reasoned that there would be a few people with only a small amount of "dust on their eyes" who might be able to understand and follow the *dhamma.* Full of confidence in the truth and efficacy of the *dhamma,* Siddhattha asked himself: "To whom should I teach the *dhamma?*" He thought first of Āḷāra Kālāma and Uddaka Rāmaputta, the two sages from whom he learned to achieve the first two stages of meditation; upon learning that both had died, he decided to search for his five ascetic companions and teach the *dhamma* to them.

Thereupon he walked towards Banāras, a sacred center where many wandering ascetics stayed during the four-month annual rainy season. On the way to Banāras a wandering ascetic named Upaka saw Siddhattha walking and questioned him. "Whose teachings do you confess?" Siddhattha replied by introducing himself as the awakened one—the Buddha.

> I have no teacher because my equal exists nowhere in the world, and I alone am quite enlightened (*buddha*). I go to Banāras now to set the wheel of *dhamma* in motion; in a blindfolded world I go to beat the deathless drum.[16]

On the outskirts of Banāras in a deer park, Buddha found the five ascetics with whom he had practiced extreme austerities. They clearly recognized Siddhattha but denounced him to each other for having abandoned their ways. Although they were initially skeptical, after approaching and hearing him expound the Four Noble Truths, they immediately became his devoted disciples and each one became enlightened soon thereafter.

For the next 45 years, Buddha traversed North India, attracting many disciples and teaching them the truth, the whole truth, and nothing but the truth about suffering, its origin, its cessation and the way leading to cessation. Buddha established monastic communities and created lay cultures regulated by a comprehensive code of conduct. He instituted disciplines designed to rid the mind of craving, the extinguishing of which is *nibbāna,* the aim and target Siddhattha hit. The accomplished archer, Siddhattha, transferred his sharp shooting skills into a mental method for hitting a higher and deeper aim.

Except for the annual rainy season during which he remained in retreat with disciples, Buddha wandered homeless with a few devoted companions, preaching peace from pain and displaying paranormal powers like reading minds, healing the sick, and walking on water and through fires, briers and walls.

Buddha contended and competed for his position against a wide range of perspectives which he called a jungle of views.[17] He tirelessly taught the Four Noble Truths, which he never asked anyone to believe simply on the basis of his authority; instead, he asked people to examine and test his teaching to verify its truth or falsity by their own experience.[18]

Buddha was a skillful teacher, effectively communicating his message to diverse people in different ways. He regarded his teachings as temporary, dispensable rafts to transport people from the sea of suffering to the shore of salvation; his teachings were simply vehicles to lead people from where they were to where he wanted them to be. Buddha was not dogmatic but diplomatic, declining to answer speculative questions about whether the universe is eternal or not, infinite or finite, whether Buddha exists after death or not, and whether the soul is the same as the body.[19] When asked why he refused to respond to these questions, Buddha answered: "I teach the *dhamma* for ending pain and suffering, for the attainment of the true goal, for realizing *nibbāna*."

Buddha was a brilliant politician who produced an institution that survived without dependence on any central leadership or location and thrived in India as long as it could sustain the support of patrons and politicians. Before his death, Buddha instructed his disciples not to appoint a successor; instead he directed them to call people to take refuge in buddha-hood, the *dhamma* (teaching) and the *sangha* (monastic community).

Death and Legacy

At age 80, feeling old, he reminded his disciples that everything changes and nothing is permanent, and admonished them to strive for their own salvation.[20]

> You must be your own lamp, be your own refuge. Take refuge in nothing outside yourselves. Hold firm to the truth as a lamp and a refuge, and do not look for refuge to anything besides yourselves. A monk becomes his own lamp and refuge by continually looking on his body, feelings, perceptions, moods and ideas in such a way that he conquers craving.[21]

Then he stretched out on his side in a reclining posture on a rope bed, and with one hand under his head and the other on his side, Buddha entered into deep meditation, where he extinguished the flickering flame of passion and final breath of life, breaking the bonds of birth and death.

Teachings

Ancient Indian philosophers typically used a medical model to articulate their position. Like a physician, Buddha formulated his Four Noble Truths in terms of disease, diagnosis, prognosis and prescription.

First Noble Truth

The first truth identifies the disease. Life is suffering. The word for suffering (*dukkha*) has a prehistory. It is an ancient Indian medical diagnosis describing the condition of a dislocated bone. The word was also used in everyday speech to describe the situation of an ox cart which wobbles when its axle is off-center from the hub of its wheel. It literally means off-center and out-of-joint, but Buddha coined the term to describe the human condition, re-minting it to mean that people are imperfect and off-center.

> The whole truth of suffering is that birth, aging, sickness, death, sorrow, disappointment, pain, grief and despair are all suffering; association with the unpleasant is suffering; separation from the pleasant is suffering; not to get what one wants is suffering; in short, life is punctuated, permeated and pervaded by suffering.[22]

The suffering of which Buddha spoke is comprehensive and characterizes the entire range of human experience, encompassing all mental and physical forms of pleasure and pain. Suffering involves mundane misery, impermanence, and the five factors of attachment.

Mundane Misery. Suffering begins with the trauma of birth, culminates in anxiety about death, and ostensibly influences and infects every experience in between. From everyday aggravations and irritations to serious psychological and physical illness, no one, even those raised in luxury like Siddhattha, can avoid facing the fact that life is full of discomfort, disappointment and dissatisfaction.

Impermanence. Suffering includes experiences of joy and happiness because they are fleeting and therefore not permanently fulfilling or totally satisfactory. The pursuit of happiness is difficult and destined to die. Nothing is permanent. Pleasures and joys are all temporary. The causes and conditions that produce all kinds of pleasant experiences are constantly changing. Pleasure often results in pain; joy can turn into sorrow and happiness to sadness. When pleasures fade, dissatisfaction follows because every experience is infected with impermanence.

Five Factors of Attachment. Human nature is constituted by a bundle of psycho-physical forces and factors of attachment that produce and perpetuate suffering. In deep meditative reflection, Buddha observed with penetrating analysis that people are composed of five identifiable, inter-dependent ingredients of attachment: material form, sensations, perceptions, mental formations, and consciousness.

The first and most foundational factor of attachment is material form which includes the body, senses, and sensory phenomena. The sensory phenomena with which the sense organs become infatuated and attached include visual shapes, sounds, odors, tastes, touches and thoughts. The mind is regarded as a sense organ which perceives thought just as the ear perceives sound. Even thoughts and mental images are regarded as material forms.

The second factor of attachment is sensations, which are the feelings that result from contact of sense organs with various material forms in the environment.

The third factor of attachment is perception, which is a subsequent stage of sensation. Sensations present the raw sensory data of experience and become perceptions when the mind recognizes or interprets them.

Human nature is comprised of sense organs which come into contact with material forms to produce sensations that become perceptions. Perceptions produce mental formations, the fourth factor of attachment, which encompass a wide range of moods, emotions, dispositions and core convictions that are manufactured by the mind, including love, hate, happiness, craving, anger, and belief in self and God, to name but a few.

The fifth factor of attachment is consciousness, which is awareness engendered and conditioned by empirical experience. Consciousness has content. It is always conscious of something. There can be no consciousness without the operation of sense organs. Consciousness, according to Buddha's rational analysis, is a function of the body. There is no disembodied consciousness; it always has discernable causes and conditions. Buddha likened consciousness to a fire. In the same way that a fire depends on its fuel for continuation, consciousness is sustained by the sensory experience on which it depends. Without fuel there can be no fire and without sensory data there can be no consciousness.

Thus the entire human experience is born, rooted and sustained in the inter-dependence of five dynamic psycho-physical factors of attachment. Buddha needed no other category of reality to explain human bondage. From head to toe, people are nothing more or less than a bundle of forces and factors of attachment, a pile of pain and suffering.[23]

Second Noble Truth

The Second Noble truth is the diagnosis that identifies craving as the cause of suffering.

> The whole truth of the origin of suffering is that craving, which produces existence and becoming, bound up with inordinate desire, discovers new delights daily, craving for sensual pleasures; craving for existence and becoming; even craving for self-annihilation.[24]

Craving is a translation of the Pali word *taṇhā*, which literally means thirst. It describes the insatiable drive with which people pursue sense pleasures, immortality and extinction. The unquenchable thirst that people have for sense pleasures expresses the same longing that some people have for eternal life and others have for permanent annihilation. The thirst for pleasure, eternal life and extinction all have the same effect: craving causes clinging to the five factors of attachment.

Thirst, *taṇhā* is one of the many mental formations mentioned above as the fourth factor of attachment. Both suffering and its cause originate in the same place. There is no need to look beyond human nature to discern and discover the cause of suffering since the whole bundle is burning with unquenchable thirst.

Third Noble Truth

The Third Noble Truth provides a promising prognosis. It postulates the complete cessation of suffering through the total eradication of craving. "The whole truth of the cessation of suffering is the complete abandonment of craving—giving it up, renouncing it, emancipating and detaching oneself from it."[25]

Fourth Noble Truth

The Fourth Noble Truth prescribes the process to destroy craving and terminate suffering. It is called the Noble Eightfold Path, also known as the Middle Way. Buddha addressed his five former ascetic companions:

Two extremes should be avoided by those who have renounced the world. What are
the two? Devotion to indulgence of sense pleasures, which is the unworthy, useless
way of ordinary people; and devotion to ascetic austerity, which is painful, profitless
and pointless. Avoiding both extremes, Buddha has realized the Middle Way, which
gives vision and knowledge, and leads to calm, insight and enlightenment.[26]

The Middle Way practiced and prescribed by Buddha is still asceticism, but a
more moderate and friendlier form than that advocated by his five companions.

The whole truth of the way leading to the cessation of suffering is the Middle Way.
And what is the Middle Way? It is the Noble Eightfold Path consisting in correct
view, correct intention, correct speech, correct action, correct career, correct effort,
correct mindfulness and correct concentration.[27]

Correct view means understanding the Four Noble Truths: life is suffering, which can be overcome by following the Middle Way to eradicate the
craving that causes it. Buddha insisted that intellectual assent is not the same
as correct understanding. It is not enough to merely affirm the Noble Truths.
Correct understanding involves an existential realization of personal suffering
caused by craving. It is complete confidence in the Middle Way. "When one
understands how material form, feeling, perception, mental formations and
consciousness are impermanent, one therein possesses correct view."[28]

Correct intention is the uncompromising resolution to seek freedom from
suffering above all else. It involves generating and radiating compassion for
the welfare of all beings. It is a complete commitment to follow the Middle
Way, resolving to pursue the prescribed path as a way of life. Practicing the
path is itself the way, truth and life.

Correct speech is motivated to promote compassion and truth, without
which one should keep Noble Silence. Buddha denounced a catalog of conversations, prohibiting rude, harsh and impolite words, gossip, idle chatter,
sarcasm, lies, slander and profanity. He taught that it is better to remain quiet
than to utter words lacking in compassion and truth.

Correct conduct refers specifically to five precepts of practice. Buddhists
vow to abstain from taking life, taking what is not given, false and misleading
speech, sexual immorality and intoxicants.

Correct career means choosing work that promotes and enhances life but
does not harm or destroy it. The sale of weapons, living beings, meat, intoxicants or poisons are among the careers Buddha prohibited because they are
not conducive to progress on the path that leads to liberation from suffering.

Correct effort refers to the diligent mental vigilance required in pursuit of the path. It is a conscientious, comprehensive and continuous mental discipline; specifically, it is the mind's energetic will to create and cultivate wholesome thoughts and to prevent and eradicate unwholesome ones.

Correct mindfulness is the deliberate direction of undivided attention to the rising and passing of physical sensations, mental moods, and emotional states within consciousness. It means cultivating an awareness that bears careful witness to psychophysical phenomena without becoming attached to or identified by them. It is a form of self-psycho-analysis which exposes, examines and eliminates the root cause of psycho-physical suffering.

Correct concentration centers the mind on a single point of focus. Sustained, uninterrupted concentration deepens into meditation in which the subject who meditates and the object of meditation become indistinguishable, engendering a unitive experience of reality. Prolonged meditation moves the mind deeper into contemplation where one discovers that there is no subject and no object, no self and no other. Enlightenment is empty of subject-object awareness; it is the realization of emptiness, the most enigmatic and misunderstood insight of Buddha. Emptiness is a translation of *suññatā*, a mathematical term signifying zero—but for Buddha emptiness is an enlightened insight into exactly how everything exists and operates. Emptiness is not the same as nothingness; it is a relational concept signaling the relationship between a container and its contents. Emptiness is the absence of something from something. But exactly what is empty of what?

Everything is empty of independence and permanence. Nothing and no one possesses either. Independence and permanence are erroneously imagined and projected onto things by unenlightened people. There is no one who exists separately or independently, and no one who exists unchanged from one moment to the next. Correct concentration culminates in enlightenment—the existential realization that frees people from attachment to the five psycho-physical forces and factors that constitute the human condition.

Between Buddha and Jesus

Between Suffering and Salvation

Buddha and Jesus both bore pain patiently, painting perfect portraits of perseverance in the face of suffering—but the suffering of which Buddha and Jesus speak is not the same. While Buddha identified craving as the cause of suffering from which people need relief, Jesus begs to differ, insisting that sin, not craving, makes salvation necessary.

Just as the Buddha's word for suffering, *dukkha,* means off-center, one of the several New Testament metaphors for sin is *hamartia,* an archery term to measure the degree by which an arrow misses the center of the target. Buddha and Jesus agree that people are missing the mark of perfection but they have radically different assessments of the human predicament. Jesus saves people, not from suffering, but from sin through suffering. For Buddha, suffering is the consequence of craving, but for Jesus separation from God is the consequence of sin.

Buddha identified craving as the immediate cause of suffering. It is the unquenchable thirst for pleasure that perpetuates the syndrome of suffering. Craving is itself a consequence of ignorance which is without beginning, though it can be eradicated. Desire and delusion generate each other like the proverbial chicken and egg. Birth is a mistake which can be corrected; it is a consequence of behavior performed in previous lives. Reincarnation is not a reward but a result of unfulfilled desires and unfinished business.

Ideas like soul and self are manufactured concepts that do not correspond to anything real.[29] Buddha used the word suffering to refer to the entire mind-body organism, insisting that there is no self or ghost in the machine; there is suffering but no self who suffers. The illusory idea of a soul which is separate from the body perpetuates attachment to a phantom figment of the imagination who becomes the suffering subject. If there is no self, what is reincarnated? The Buddha's answer is thirst, craving, the energetic will to be, to become more and more.

Jesus and Buddha both pointed people beyond the superficial self with its images and interests to an inner quality of life that transcends self-centricity, but Buddha denies reality to the self that Jesus came to save. Doctrinal denial of a self is not the same as self-denial. Buddha claims there is no self, but Jesus says there is a self and only those who lose it for his sake will find it.[30] The saga of salvation is the story of the self, lost and found.

The Middle Way that Buddha walked to alleviate suffering crisscrosses but does not completely coincide with the way, truth, and life that Jesus claimed to be. While Buddha prescribed the Middle Way as the means to eradicate thirst, Jesus presented himself as the living water which wells up into eternal life to fully satisfy the deepest longings of those who drink it. Whereas Buddha preached a path of disciplined self-effort, Jesus told his disciples: "I am the vine and you are the branches. Those who abide in me bear much fruit but apart from me you can do nothing."[31]

Jesus is the suffering servant, not eradicating suffering, but enduring and embracing it on behalf of others as the way of salvation itself. Jesus charged his disciples to suffer for his sake. "Anyone who wants to be my disciple must deny themselves, take up their cross and follow me."[32] Taking up a cross is the resolve to live and die for Jesus and to voluntarily suffer ridicule, rejection and persecution along the way.

> If the world hates you, keep in mind that it hated me first. If you belonged to the world, it would love you as its own. As it is, you do not belong to the world, but I have chosen you out of the world. That is why the world hates you. Remember what I told you: "A servant is not greater than his master," If they persecuted me, they will persecute you also.[33]

Between *Nibbāna* and Eternal Life

Nibbāna is the annihilation of all craving that leads to suffering.[34] When asked about *nibbāna*, one of Buddha's disciples answered: "Whatever is the cessation of greed, hatred and delusion, this is called *nibbāna*."[35] It literally means extinguished; *nibbāna* is the condition of a candle blown out. Buddha used the word metaphorically in reference to a person who has extinguished the fire and quenched the thirst that is craving.[36] *Nibbāna* is freedom from craving and the cycle of reincarnation that it perpetuates. It is difficult to describe in words because there is nothing that can be positively predicated about it. It was easier for Buddha to say what it was not.

> There is, o' monks, an unborn, not become, unproduced, not compounded. Were it not for this, no escape from the born, become, produced and compounded would be known. But since there is an unborn, not-become, unproduced, not-compounded, there is an escape.[37]

Nibbāna exists but is not the result of any causes. It is not brought about as a consequence of following the Middle Way any more than a mountain peak is created by the trail one takes to reach it. *Nibbāna* just is. It is to be realized, not created or brought into being as a result of efforts and actions. It is ever present and available, accessible and attainable through the diligent, disciplined practice of the Middle Way. In brief, *nibbāna* is freedom from suffering, which one realizes when the causes of suffering are extinguished.

According to Buddha, yearning for eternal life is an expression of the very same craving which leads to suffering. Buddha regarded the desire to live forever as an unfulfillable craving. Jesus begs to differ, claiming himself to be eternal life. In the final hours before his arrest, Jesus prayed:

> Father the hour has come. Glorify your Son that your Son may glorify you. For you granted him authority over all people that he might give eternal life to all those you have given him. Now this is eternal life: that they know you, the one true God and Jesus Christ, whom you have sent.[38]

What Christians Might Learn From Buddha

Meditation

Christians can learn a practical technique for meditation from Buddha. Buddhist meditative method can be adopted and adapted to achieve single-pointed concentration for contemplation and prayer. Meditation, according to Buddha, begins with attention to the breath. By fixing one's undivided attention on breathing through the nose, the heart rate slows and a sense of tranquility settles the mind for deeper contemplation. By practicing this procedure, Christians may find they are able to calm and focus their minds in ways that heighten awareness of God's presence in prayer. "Then the Lord God formed a man from the dust of the ground and breathed into his nostrils the breath of life, and man became a living being."[39]

The word meditation comes into English from the Latin verb *meditatio*, a term to describe the activity of a cow chewing her cud. It is a picturesque word, envisioning the redundancy of recurring cycles of chewing, swallowing, and regurgitating, only to repeat the process until all the valuable nutrients are fully infused and digested.

Mindful meditation on Scripture provides spiritual nourishment. The Scriptures not only endorse meditation, they are an instrument of meditation itself. The Psalmist exclaims, "Oh, how I love your law; I meditate on it all day long."[40] Jesus said: "It is written: man shall not live on bread alone but on every word that comes from the mouth of God."[41] Scripture is spiritual milk but the only way to procure its nourishment is by meditation. Christian meditation is rumination on Scripture. It begins with memorization which is itself a form of meditation. What is not known by heart cannot be pondered by the mind.

Notes

1. *Cullavagga* 11.1.1 *of Vinaya, The Book of Discipline* (*Vinaya Pitika*) translated by I. E. Horner, Forgotten Books, 2018.

2. *Aṅguttara Nikāya* 3:38. Bodhi, Bhikkhu, *Numerical Discourses of Buddha: A Translation of the Aṅguttara Nikāya*, Wisdom Publications, 2012. All references to the *Aṅguttara Nikāya* are based on this translation unless otherwise noted.

3. *Sutta Nipāta* 3:11; translated by Saddhatissa, Curzon Press, 1994.

4. *Aṅguttara Nikāya* 3.

5. *Aṅguttara Nikāya* 3:38.

6. *Majjhima Nikāya* 26. Nanamoli, Bhikkhu, *The Middle Length Discourses of Buddha: A Translation of the Majjhima Nikāya*, Wisdom Publications, 1995. All references to the *Majjhima Nikāya* are based on this translation unless otherwise noted.

7. *Aṅguttara Nikāya* 3:38.

8. *Majjhima Nikāya* 36, 100.

9. *Majjhima Nikāya* 26, 36, 85, 100.

10. *Majjhima Nikāya* 26.

11. *Majjhima Nikāya* 26.

12. *Majjhima Nikāya* 36, 85, 100.

13. *Majjhima Nikāya* 36, 85, 100.

14. *Majjhima Nikāya* 36, 85, 100.

15. *Majjhima Nikāya* 36.

16. *Mahavagga of the Vinaya* 1:6, *The Book of the Discipline* (*Vinaya Pitika*), translated by I. E. Horner, Forgotten Books, 2018; *Majjhima Nikāya* 26, 85.

17. *Majjhima Nikāya* 2.

18. *Aṅguttara Nikāya* 1:189.

19. *Aṅguttara Nikāya* 10:95.

20. *Aṅguttara Nikāya* 4:76; *Mahāparinibbāna Sutta of the Dīgha Nikāya*, translated by Maurice Walshe, Wisdom Publications 2012. All references to the *Mahāparinibbāna Sutta* are from this translation unless otherwise noted.

21. *Mahāparinibbāna Sutta.*

22. *Saṃyutta Nikāya* 56:11. Bodhi, Bhikkhu, *The Connected Discourses of Buddha: A Translation of the Saṃyutta Nikāya*, Wisdom Publications, 2000. All references to the *Saṃyutta Nikāya* are based on this translation.

23. *Saṃyutta Nikāya* 22:26, 48, 56.

24. *Saṃyutta Nikāya* 22:26, 48, 56.

25. *Saṃyutta Nikāya* 56:2.

26. *Saṃyutta Nikāya* 56:2.

27. *Saṃyutta Nikāya* 56:2.

28. *Saṃyutta Nikāya* 22:51; 35:155.

29. *Saṃyutta Nikāya* 22:59; 44:10.

30. *Luke* 17:33, *Holy Bible: New International Version*, Zondervan Publishers, 1984. All Bible references are based on this translation unless otherwise noted.

31. *John* 15:5.

32. *Matthew* 16:24.
33. *John* 15:18–20.
34. *Aṅguttara Nikāya* 10:60.
35. *Saṃyutta Nikāya* 4:251.
36. *Udāna* 8:1–4, Strong, D. M., *The Udāna: A Translation of the Solemn Utterances of Buddha*, Forgotten Books, 2016.
37. *Udāna* 81, Strong, D. M., *The Udāna: A Translation of the Solemn Utterances of Buddha*, Forgotten Books, 2016.
38. *John* 17:3.
39. *Genesis* 2:7.
40. *Psalms* 119:97.
41. *Matthew* 4:4.

· 3 ·

KŖṢŅA

Introduction

Of the proverbial 333,000,000 divinities worshipped in India, Kṛṣṇa is by far the most popular and beloved. He is among the most renowned and revered religious figures in the world. Some Hindus adore him as an incarnation of Viṣṇu, the preserver of the world; while others regard Kṛṣṇa as the supreme transcendent ruler of the universe who appears on earth to rescue the world by intervening whenever the cosmic and social order is threatened by demonic, despotic forces. "I come into being age after age to protect the virtuous and to destroy evil-doers, to establish a firm basis for the true eternal order."[1]

Literary references to the worship of a divine Kṛṣṇa date back to the fifth century BCE, and artifacts unearthed by archaeologists establish evidence of his footprints in ancient India. Historical verifiability for Kṛṣṇa also comes from Megasthenes, a fourth century BCE Greek ambassador to the court of Indian emperor Chandragupta Maurya. Megasthenes wrote a book describing his observations in India titled *Indika* and, although it did not survive, it was quoted by three enduring Greek sources who describe details also confirming the presence of Kṛṣṇa worship in India hundreds of years before Christ.

The Greek historian Quintus Curtius records that Alexander the Great encountered the Indian army of King Porus, whose soldiers paraded an image of Kṛṣṇa at the front of their flanks. Additional evidence in the form of an inscription on the Heliodorus column from the first century BCE confirms that a Greek diplomatic envoy to India had been converted to the worship of Vasudeva Kṛṣṇa, whom they revered as the God of gods.

Text-historical scholars delineate three Kṛṣṇa's who correspond to the different texts which detail his life and teachings.[2] The texts not only represent distinct historical situations and socio-economic conditions but they also present their own versions and visions of Kṛṣṇa that are not readily reconciled into a chronologically coherent character. Despite disparate sources, Hindu popular piety recognizes a single compound, complex character called Vasudeva Kṛṣṇa.

Kṛṣṇa inherited a culture of complex ideas about the relationship between the world, humanity and ultimate reality. Just as the life and teachings of Jesus are presented in relationship to themes introduced in the Hebrew Bible, Kṛṣṇa is presented in the context of older sacred Sanskrit textual traditions.

Socio-political Context

Veda

India's oldest extant sacred scripture, the *Veda*, which means wisdom, reveals the secret knowledge necessary for priestly sacrifices (*yajña*), the success of which upholds the world and fulfills human needs. Composed in Sanskrit and compiled over several centuries, the *Veda* is traditionally regarded as the revelation of ultimate reality in eternal, authorless words.

The *Veda* includes ritual formulae called *mantras* which reveal the reciprocal nature and structure of reality and provide the ritual regulations and procedures necessary to maintain social and cosmic order. *Vedic* ritual sacrifice is a proto-science operating on a principle of correspondence and identity between arenas of ritual performance and realms of power. The success of *Vedic* sacrifice depends on its correct performance by ritual specialists called *brahmins*, who are custodians of the ritual's efficacious power called *Brahman*.

The principle purpose of *Vedic* sacrifice is to sustain the world by empowering the various agents responsible for maintaining the social and cosmic order. Sacrifice is the source of power on which the cosmos, gods, kings, and people depend. The sacrificial ritual space is a sacred sphere where gods, priests and patrons share food. Sacrifice is the transaction necessary to sustain life. It entails relinquishing something for the benefit of someone else. Food comes from once living things which are sacrificed to sustain others. Living beings are sustained by the death of other beings. The universe continues to operate due to sacrifices. Thus the *Vedic* sacrificial ritual mirrors the universe as a reciprocal production and consumption through which it perpetuates and sustains itself. Krsna claims to be the sacred sacrifice itself and also the only real recipient of all sacrifices.

> Even those who are devotees of other gods, and sacrifice to them full of faith, really sacrifice to me. For I am the Lord and the recipient of all sacrifices, though they fail to recognize me and fall.[3]

An ancient *Vedic* hymn poetically portrays the creation of the universe as a dramatic cosmic sacrifice.[4] An eternal person without origin called *Purusa*, sacrifices itself in an act of divine dismemberment, transforming and distributing its anatomy into the various dimensions of cosmic and social order. The hymn correlates various parts of *Purusa's* anatomy to different dimensions of the cosmos and society.

On the social level *Purusa's* mouth became the priests who utter *mantras*, ritual formulae required to access and appropriate the power of the sacrifice and secure its successful results. From *Purusa's* arms came soldiers and kings who wield weapons in shouldering their responsibility to protect the world, promote prosperity, preserve the peace, and protect the social order. From *Purusa's* thighs came society's farmers, artisans, and merchants, who are producers of food and material support. Last, but no less integral to the harmonious functioning of the socio-economic order, from *Purusa's* feet came servants, the menial laborers who provide the vital services on which all levels of society stand. Krsna claims to be the architect, protector and upholder of the social and cosmic order.[5]

Careful analysis of the hymn reveals the principle of reciprocity as central to the sacrificial nature and structure of the universe. *Purusa* is identified with the entire universe itself and beyond, providing the *Vedic* vision of a supreme God who both fills the universe and is simultaneously transcendent to it. The universe in turn is identified as the sacrifice itself. Not merely a metaphor, sacrifice is the very structure, movement, and meaning of the universe. From the sacrifice of *Purusa*, everything is created and sustained. Krsna identifies himself as the sacrifice that sustains the cosmic and social order, and *Purusa* is his creative agency.

Upaniṣads

Reflecting on the meaning of sacrifice, sages sought spiritual union with the source of its power. Through rigorous ritual reasoning, poet priests and sages composed discussions and dialogues on the symbolic structure and inner meaning of the sacrificial ritual. These discourses were compiled into texts that became known as *Upaniṣads*, which means to sit down near, depicting the proximity and posture of a student interacting with a teacher.

Having identified *Puruṣa* or *Brahman* as the ultimate power of the universe which makes the sacrificial ritual effective, the sages turned their contemplative gaze inward in search of that same principle and power operative in their own being. Looking within through methods of meditation, the sages discovered that humans are layered beings. By introspective analysis, sages discovered that the innermost core of their being was identical to the infinite power of the sacrifice, *Puruṣa* or *Brahman*.

The innermost-self is called *Ātman*, which is a reflexive pronoun meaning myself. It refers to the profound, pure self which is different from the various levels and layers of the psycho-physical organism that it animates and inhabits. *Upaniṣadic* sages revealed the secret that *Ātman is Brahman*, the infinite beyond is accessible and discoverable within. In light of the profound insight which equates the innermost-self with the ultimate power of the universe, meditative techniques were developed as means through which to realize and experience the union of *Ātman* and *Brahman*.

The *Upaniṣads* reveal insights about the nature of humans and their relationship to the world, which evolves from nature called *Prakṛti*, infinite materiality without beginning or end. Before each creative cycle of evolution, *Prakṛti* exists in an invisible potential state. From a single substance, the entire world has evolved and differentiated itself into a multiplicity of dynamic interactions. The reason the world evolves from an invisible material potentiality is for the sake of *Puruṣa*, which is non-material, pure consciousness. Like *Prakṛti*, *Puruṣa* is infinite and without beginning or end. *Prakṛti* is matter or nature and *Puruṣa* is spirit or consciousness, which does not share any of the characteristics of *Prakṛti*. *Prakṛti* is excited and induced into its evolutionary process by the mere presence of *Puruṣa*.

When an individual is born, *Puruṣa* becomes embodied, entangled and imprisoned in *Prakṛti*. Yoga is the process through which a person gradually and systematically shifts identity from the psycho-physical self, centered in the sense of I, me and mine, to the transcendent spiritual self which is found deep within and characterized by infinite being, awareness and bliss.

Response and reaction to *Vedic* sacrificial ritual and *Upaniṣadic* meditative traditions ranged from outright rejection to innovative adaptation and radical reinterpretation. Mahāvīra and Buddha flatly denied the authority of *Vedic* revelation and rejected the validity of its religion but developed their own distinctive forms of philosophy and meditative practice in contradistinction to it. Kṛṣṇa, as we will see, radically reinterpreted the *Vedic* tradition in light of himself as the supreme yogi and ideal king of the universe, exalted high above the Vedic sacrifice, *Puruṣa*, and even the mystical union of *Ātman-Brahman*.

Texts as Context

Mahābhārata and *Bhagavad Gītā*

India's original and traditional name is the land of *Bharata*, the name of India's primeval, prototypical king, and the *Mahābhārata* is the epic that culminates in the great battle for dominion of India between two families descended from King *Bharata*. The *Mahābhārata* is an epic poem of about 100,000 verses composed and compiled in many layers over hundreds of years beginning in the fifth century BCE through its final redaction by the third century of the common era.

The *Bhagavad Gītā*—song of God—is a poetic dialogue between Kṛṣṇa and a warrior prince named Arjuna through whom Kṛṣṇa teaches his universal message to the world. The *Bhagavad Gītā* (hereafter referred to as *Gītā*) may have been composed over several centuries contiguously in concert with the central theme of the *Mahābhārata* into which it was integrated. The *Gītā* is the culmination and climax of events narrated in the *Mahābhārata*.

From one particular historical perspective the *Gītā* can be read as a protest against kings who claimed to possess absolute power. It can also be interpreted as an apologetic for how heroic soldiers, kings and princes can avoid the negative consequences of violence necessitated by their roles as warrior-protectors of the people.[6] The *Gītā* promises blessings to those who memorize, recite and expound it but prohibits its secret to be taught to people who are disinterested or antagonistic to Kṛṣṇa. Its message is at once a universalization of salvation and an affirmation of the *Vedic* socio-political status quo.

Bhāgavata Purāṇa

The *Bhāgavata Purāṇa* is part of a corpus of literature known collectively as *Puranas*, meaning prior or older, implying that they describe events at least as old as the creation of the world. Historically the *Puranas* were composed after the *Veda* yet each *Purana* claims to be an authoritative and succinct summary of *Vedic* revelation for a particular time and place; the *Bhāgavata Purāṇa* claims to surpass the *Veda* because of its superior revelation of Kṛṣṇa as the ultimate reality.

A biography of Kṛṣṇa's life occupies the 10th book of the *Bhāgavata Purāṇa*, a ninth century Sanskrit scripture which claims to embody Kṛṣṇa himself, enabling listeners to vicariously experience his presence through hearing about his divine activity or *līlā*, God's play or pastimes. The ninth book presents a succinct summary of his life:

> Born as son of Vasudeva and Devaki, Kṛṣṇa departed from his parents to Vrindavan in order to gladden its residents. He killed his enemies, accepted many excellent wives, and begat hundreds of sons by them. The supreme person Kṛṣṇa, worshipped himself by sacrificial rites and spread his own teachings among the people. Then, by inducing enmity among the Kauravas, who had become a great burden on the earth, Kṛṣṇa caused them to be destroyed. By his mere glance on the royal armies, he purged them in battle and declared victory for the Pāṇḍavas. Finally after teaching Arjuna, he proceeded to his supreme abode.[7]

Variant biographies of Kṛṣṇa are contained in the *Harivamsa*, an early appendix to the *Mahābhārata*, and in the *Viṣṇu Purana*, a first century sectarian text of a Hindu tradition that regards Kṛṣṇa as a form of Viṣṇu rather than vice-versa. In the interest of composing a coherent, consistent, composite biography, we begin with Kṛṣṇa's youth and childhood as narrated in the *Bhāgavata Purāṇa* and move backwards to discover the purpose of his mission and the meaning of his message delivered in the *Mahābhārata* and *Gītā*.

Birth and Youth

Kṛṣṇa was born in a prison in Mathura, an ancient and enduring North Indian city, several millennia before Jesus appeared in a barn in Bethlehem.[8] King Kamsa, Kṛṣṇa's maternal uncle, learned by a revelation that one of his sister's children would grow up to kill him. The king, full of fear and hatred, threw his sister and her husband into prison and murdered every child they bore there except for Kṛṣṇa, whose parents snuck him out of the prison and arranged to have him smuggled into the nearby village of Vrindavan. There he was raised by Nandā, chief of the village cowherders, and his wife Yaśodā.

When the evil tyrant, King Kamsa, learned that his sister's son and would-be assassin was alive in Vrindavan, he tried but repeatedly failed to kill Kṛṣṇa. The first attempt the king sent a demoness in the guise of a beautiful wet-nurse who doted over the infant and offered to breastfeed him. Knowing she intended to kill him with poison from her bosom, the baby suckled the life out of the demoness and, to the king's chagrin, liberated her soul in salvation.[9]

Next, the king dispatched a demon in the form of a tornado that whisked the child away, whirling him high into the air. Kṛṣṇa, exerting his paranormal power to become unbearably heavy, clutched hold of the demon's neck and forced him to drop like a stone, shattering all over the ground.[10]

Divine Juvenile Delinquency

As a child Kṛṣṇa was a notorious prankster.[11] He shamelessly stole butter from kitchens and fed it to monkeys. No one seemed to mind his mischievous manners; instead everyone indulged the enchanting child in all his juvenile delinquency and dalliance.

In Vrindavan, Kṛṣṇa endeared himself to the young cowherd boys, stealing their hearts and minds, infatuating them with his boyish, childhood charm. He cunningly convinced his cow herding companions to perform an annual *Vedic* ritual sacrifice to a local hill instead of its intended recipient Indra, *Vedic* god of rain and war.[12] Indra, angered and enraged by the neglect and usurpation of his worship, vented his wrath, trouncing and threatening to drown all the inhabitants and their cows in a torrential downpour. In a dramatic display of divine personality and power, Kṛṣṇa lifted the hill with a single finger, raising it as an umbrella above the village to provide shelter from the storm and protection from the fury of an irate Indra. Kṛṣṇa thereby demonstrated his supremacy over nature, *Vedic* gods, and cosmic powers.[13]

Divine Lover

As a handsome youth, Kṛṣṇa, with the mystical music of his flute, lured the lovely milk-maids of Vrindavan out of their marriage beds into the forest. There he danced and simultaneously made love with them in such a way that each thought she alone was the object of his exclusive affection and undivided attention, intimating God's personal and intimate love for each individual devotee.[14]

Kṛṣṇa's *līlā* with the milk maids is not sexual but a symbolic spiritual expression of the intimate, reciprocal love relationship between Kṛṣṇa and his devotees, who are willing to abandon marriage norms and risk social criticism for the sake of loving devotion to Kṛṣṇa. The *līlā* of love demonstrates that devotion to Kṛṣṇa transcends social rules and roles but is not at odds with them. All social roles and responsibilities are to be performed as sacrificial acts of devotional service to Kṛṣṇa. The low social status of the milk maids demonstrates Kṛṣṇa's democratization of devotion, making salvation accessible to all regardless of social standing; this is in sharp contrast to *Vedic* traditions which restricted ritual access to liberation on the basis of social standing. "For whoever depends on me, however low their origins—whether they are women, farmers and merchants, or even common laborers and servants—they go by the highest path."[15]

On another occasion, a group of *Vedic* priests' wives heard the alluring sound of Kṛṣṇa's flute and left their marriage beds to seek his love in the forest. In respect to social norms, Kṛṣṇa sent the women back to their husbands with the assurance that they would not be socially criticized or morally condemned. Kṛṣṇa taught them that they could enjoy the divine play of love through single-minded meditation on him from home, clearly establishing that love play symbolizes a spiritual encounter with Kṛṣṇa. The text unequivocally states that participation in Kṛṣṇa's love play frees people from lust and establishes them in loving devotion. The women's husbands envied their wives for the intimacy they had attained with Kṛṣṇa, especially poignant in view of the fact that their *Vedic* tradition provided no ritual paths to liberation for women.

Assassination Attempts

King Kamsa, having already failed two assassination attempts, commissioned a demon to appear as a calf, which Kṛṣṇa took by the tail and tossed into a tree.[16] Next, the king dispatched a demon incarnated as a crane which swallowed the beautiful young Kṛṣṇa, who invoked his paranormal yogic power to become exceedingly hot, compelling the bird to vomit him out. Kṛṣṇa then playfully ripped the demon crane to shreds.[17] The king sent yet another demon, which appeared as an enormous snake whose mouth covered the earth and extended to the sky. Its fangs looked like mountain peaks to Kṛṣṇa's beguiled playmates, who were unwittingly lured into its mouth. In order to rescue his friends, Kṛṣṇa allowed the snake to swallow him. Appropriating his paranormal ability to grow infinitesimally large, Kṛṣṇa gradually increased in size until he tore the snake apart from within.[18] Kṛṣṇa also defeated demons in the form of donkeys, which he took by their tails and dashed into palm trees, and a bull, which he grabbed by the horns and squeezed to death between his knees.[19] Krsna killed a would-be assassin in the form of an attacking demonic horse by shoving his fist down its throat and making his arm grow so large that the horse choked to death.[20]

Krsna's final victory over demons in Vrindavan was against the many-headed sea serpent living in a nearby stream. The serpent was poisoning the people's water supply and terrorizing the town. When Krsna learned of the serpent's treachery, he climbed a tree, jumped into the stream, and playfully splashed to attract the sea creature. At first, Krsna permitted the sea monster to gain the upper hand, allowing himself to be gripped in its tentacles. But the beautiful youth soon turned the tables by whirling and twirling, dazzling and dizzying the demon into exhaustion. He danced and pranced on its many heads until the dastardly demon pleaded for mercy.[21]

Mission

Krsna redeems the demons by defeating them, displaying the paranormal powers of a yogi. The purpose of Krsna's life in Vrindavan is play; however, when Krsna departs Vrindavan, his youth transforms into adulthood and his mission becomes more deliberate. In Vrindavan, the demons he defeated were impositions but not disruptions, innovatively incorporated into his divine play. He faces and defeats them in spontaneous sport. However, when Krsna departs Vrindavan to confront King Kamsa in Mathura, he leaves his child play behind and becomes a man of heroic valor who deliberately and dutifully seeks out demonic and despotic kings to conquer and kill.

The *Mahābhārata* presents Krsna as God in the role of diplomat who devises strategies to defeat demonic armies which terrorize the world, and the *Gītā* reveals Krsna as God in the role of teacher of wisdom and truth to humanity. There is no *līlā* in the *Gītā*, no playful pastimes. All three texts depict God with a mission. Krsna's purposeful play and serious mission to maintain social order are not at odds with each other; he reconciles performance of social responsibilities for the welfare of the world with liberation from it.

Defeat of Despotism and Departure

Krsna returned to Mathura, where he vanquished the cruel King Kamsa in a wrestling match and restored temporary peace to the realm.[22] After deposing

King Kamsa of Mathura in the *Bhāgavata Purāṇa*, we track and trace Kṛṣṇa in the *Mahābhārata* as King of Dvaraka, a North Indian kingdom. Kṛṣṇa was cousin and ally to both rival factions of the disputing descendants of King Bharata. Members of the two rival families debated among themselves over the necessity for war. Famous for his skill in statesmanship, Kṛṣṇa was called upon to negotiate a peace settlement between the rival families, but due to the obstinate King Duryodhana's determination to defend and extend his kingdom, even at the demise of his family, war became unavoidable.

Sometime shortly after the 18-day battle in which the despotic Duryo-dhana was defeated, Kṛṣṇa escorted Arjuna and the few surviving victors on a journey to his celestial abode. On their way, however, Kṛṣṇa was accidentally wounded by an arrow shot from the bow of a hunter who mistook him for a deer.[23] With his final breath, Kṛṣṇa forgave the hunter, assured him it was all meant to be, then smiled and slipped into a meditative trance from which he voluntarily ascended to his celestial abode.

Teachings

For Kṛṣṇa's message we turn to the *Gītā*, whose context is the battlefield on which two rival, related families, the Pāṇḍavas and the Kauravas, are assembled to fight for political dominion. In the section of the *Mahābhārata* that immediately precedes the *Gītā*, Duryodhana, king of the Kauravas, has exalted himself as an absolute monarch, above even the gods and priests of the *Vedic* sacrifice.

Having failed to negotiate a peaceful settlement between the families and faced with the inevitability of impending war, Kṛṣṇa refused to take sides or carry a weapon, though he offered the fractured families a choice between employing his armed forces or engaging his personal council. The Pāṇḍavas chose Kṛṣṇa's council, which he rendered by assuming the role of charioteer and advisor to the family's champion archer and prince, Arjuna. The Kauru-vas, led by the despotic Duryodhana, received the aide of Kṛṣṇa's army.

As Arjuna surveyed the enemy from his chariot, he saw his uncles, cous-ins, friends and teachers among the opposition.[24] His mind and heart reeled and reasoned that it made no sense to win a kingdom by killing the very people he loved. The soldier had a serious ethical dilemma. On the one hand, he is a warrior-prince whose social responsibility is to protect society, but he also has a moral obligation and duty to respect his family and friends, who are

assembled and ready to do battle against him. It is a conflict between fidelity
to family and loyalty to his responsibility as a soldier: Arjuna complains:

> How can we be so ignorant as not to recoil from this wrong? The evil incurred by
> destroying one's family is plain to see.[25] We are about to perpetuate a great evil—out
> of sheer greed for kingdoms and pleasures, we are prepared to kill our own people.[26]

The otherwise brave fighter, Arjuna suddenly became a conscientious objec-
tor to war and violence, proclaiming it would be better to be killed in battle
unarmed and unresisting.[27] Overwhelmed, Arjuna slumped down in his chariot and defiantly declared: "I will not fight."[28]

Krsna chides Arjuna for timidity in the face of adversity: "Arjuna, where
do you get this weakness from at a time of crisis? Abandon this inner weakness and get up."[29] Nevertheless, Arjuna protests: "How can I shoot arrows at
my own family whom I should be honoring, not killing?"[30] Krsna responds to
Arjuna's despondency by consoling him with the doctrine of the eternal soul
and reincarnation.

Reincarnation and the Soul

> Wise men do not grieve for the dead or the living. Never was there a time when I
> did not exist, nor you nor any of these men, and never shall any of us cease to exist
> hereafter. Just as the embodied self passes through childhood, youth and old age in
> this body, in the same manner it will obtain another body.[31]

According to Krsna, each individual soul is absolutely eternal, without beginning or end. For this reason, says Krsna, there is no cause for grief when someone dies. Only the body perishes—but not the soul. After death, the soul
reincarnates through a perpetual process of rebirth into different bodies until
it finds final liberation and release from the syndrome of rebirth and re-death.
Moreover, Krsna assures Arjuna that there is no guilt accruing to the soldier
who performs his duty:

> He who thinks the embodied self a slayer and he who imagines it is slain, neither of
> these understand. It does not slay, nor is it slain. It is never born, and it never dies.
> Like a person who has cast off old clothes and puts on others that are new, thus the
> embodied-self casts off old bodies and moves onto others that are new.[32]

In light of the doctrine of reincarnation, Krsna counsels Arjuna not to be concerned about such conflicts of conscience in the face of battle: "Recognizing

your inherent duty, you must not shrink from it. For there is nothing better for a warrior than a duty-bound war."[33] Kṛṣṇa tells Arjuna exactly how to fight: "Making yourself indifferent to pleasure and pain, gain and loss, victory and defeat, commit yourself to battle. In that way, you will not violate your duty."[34]

The *Vedic* warrior code required soldiers to carry out their military duties with indifference to personal concerns for wealth or well-being. If they died, they inherited a hero's reward in paradise; if they survived in victory, they enjoyed honor and the fruit of their conquest here on earth.[35] Indifference to personal gain or loss was central to the warrior's code and fostered heroic bravery in battle, but even detached, disinterested action needs a motive and purpose. The purpose of soldiers and kings is to protect society and promote its prosperity. Normally, Arjuna's duty as a warrior would not conflict with his duty to family. His success as a soldier ordinarily protects his family and helps it to prosper, but this situation is different. He is commanded to fight and kill his own relatives. In existential anguish, Arjuna asks Kṛṣṇa to explain why it would not be better to renounce the world and avoid action altogether.

In response, Kṛṣṇa teaches Arjuna that inaction is not an option because action is inherent to nature (*Prakṛti*). Inaction is impossible, and those who pride themselves on a total renunciation of action only delude themselves because they are compelled to act by the forces of nature itself. Even renouncers of the world must perform actions to maintain themselves. Kṛṣṇa further explains the law of social responsibility to Arjuna:

> You have an obligation to perform social duty but no entitlement to its results. You must be neither motivated by the results of action nor attached to inaction. For action in itself is inferior by far to yogic discipline. The person disciplined in yoga renounces in this world the results of both good and evil actions. Therefore commit yourself to yogic discipline, which is skill in actions.[36]

The heroic warrior and the yogi renouncer are both disinterested actors. The soldier acts altruistically for the maintenance of the world while the yogi performs disciplines for liberation from it. Kṛṣṇa teaches Arjuna yoga: "Restraining all senses, one should sit in yogic discipline, focused on me; for if one's senses are under control, one's mentality is grounded."[37]

Still, Arjuna does not see how practicing yoga is the solution to his moral crisis. He protests: "Kṛṣṇa, if it is your belief that yoga is superior to action, then why do you direct me to do this terrible undertaking?"[38] Arjuna is deeply perplexed and asks Kṛṣṇa to remove his confusion and clarify the teaching.

In response, Krsna reveals himself to Arjuna as the original teacher of a royal yoga, a secret knowledge of kings that has been passed on in an unbroken lineage until it was temporarily lost. Krsna's teaching restores the secret royal knowledge of yoga to Arjuna, and through him to the world. "Therefore without attachment, always do whatever action has to be done; for it is through acting without attachment that a person attains the highest. Looking only to what maintains the world, you too must act."[39]

The Problem of Karma

Krsna's philosophy of salvation provides his unique solution to the problem of *karma*, the cause of recurring births and deaths. *Karma*, in this context, means the universal, transcendent law of action. Every action in the moral realm has a corresponding consequence. Virtuous actions produce positive results while immoral actions generate negative ones. But the problem with all actions, good and bad, is that they create consequences which the actor must live to face and experience sooner or later, in this life or a future one. Actions bind the actor to the results.

Reincarnation is not India's version of immortality; this vicious cycle of birth and death, compelled by *karma*, is the syndrome of suffering from which each Indian religion proposes its own particular path of salvation.

The Yoga of Devotion

Krsna's solution to the problem of *karma* and its consequences is clear: the only way to avoid producing personal consequences is to perform actions dutifully as sacrificial rituals in devotion to Krsna without any attachment to the results. Performance of social roles and responsibilities are for the sake of maintaining the world because it is Krsna's creation and the object of his affection. Devotion to Krsna is both the way and the goal of salvation from the otherwise endless rounds of birth and death.

The aim of worshipping Krsna is to destroy attachments to the world by redirecting affections and desires to him. As devotion to Krsna increases, attachment to the world decreases and release from the clutches of *karma* becomes possible. Devotion is the way by which a person gradually transcends self-centeredness, seeks Krsna as life's highest aim, and longs for eternal communion with him. Krsna teaches that all actions are to be performed as worship in a spirit of self-sacrifice, which means acting without expecting anything in return.

By sacrificing actions and their results to Kṛṣṇa in a spirit of selfless non-attachment, devotees induce Kṛṣṇa's grace. Renunciation of social roles and responsibilities is not necessary for salvation because real renunciation is not a repudiation of social actions but total abandonment of all desire to benefit from the results.

> It is the person who performs ritual action, without depending on the results of that action, who is a renouncer and a yogi, not the one who has renounced the world. For the person who has renounced all intention to obtain a particular result, and clings neither to actions nor to the objects of senses, has attained yogic discipline.[40]

The way of salvation does not demand denial of daily duties but calls for a radical change of mentality and motivation toward performing them. Devotion is action done without desire for reward and motivated by love of God.

> The person whose self is disciplined in yoga, whose perception is the same everywhere, sees their self in all creatures and all creatures in their self. For the person who sees me in everything and everything in me, is not lost to me, nor I to them.[41]

Despite all this instruction in yoga, Arjuna is still confounded, confesses that he does not see the oneness of which Kṛṣṇa speaks, and concedes that his mind is unsteady and as difficult to restrain as the wind. Kṛṣṇa empathizes with Arjuna but reassures him that by repeated practice and by cultivating indifference to passion, the mind can be held in check.[42] He promises Arjuna:

> Practicing yogic discipline with your mind intent on me, dependent on me, you shall know me entirely and unreservedly. I shall tell you in full about this knowledge and insight; once you know this, nothing more remains to be known in this world.[43]

Kṛṣṇa's Self Disclosure

Kṛṣṇa reveals himself as the only necessary object of knowledge for liberation. He explains that the entire creation is his lower nature (*Prakṛti*) and his higher nature (*Puruṣa*) sustains the universe.

> There is nothing at all higher than me; all this is strung on me like pearls on a thread. The entire universe is deluded by nature and is not aware of me, eternal and beyond nature. For it is hard to go beyond this divine appearance of mine; only those who turn to me alone overcome this appearance. Clothed in the appearance created by my own yogic power, I am not clearly visible to all; this deluded world does not recognize me as unchanging and unborn.[44]

However, he reveals to Arjuna that "for the perpetually disciplined yogi who continuously thinks on me, and whose mind is never anywhere else, I am easy to reach. And once I am reached, rebirth is finished."[45]

Krṣna reveals himself as the secret royal knowledge: "Fix your mind on me; and so devoted to me, sacrificing to me, reverencing me, having disciplined yourself, with me as your final resort, you shall come to me."[46]

> Whoever truly knows this revealed all-pervading power and yoga of mine is disciplined by an unshakable yoga about which there can be no doubt. The wise, filled with my state of being, share in me, knowing that I am the origin of all this, and that everything unrolls from me. To those who are continuously disciplined, who worship me full of joy, I grant the discipline of yoga by which they come to me. Situated in their being, out of compassion for them I dispel the darkness born of their ignorance with the bright lamp of knowledge.[47]

Arjuna responds by confessing faith in the essential truth of all that Krṣna has said and requests a complete catalogue of divine attributes on which to meditate for obtaining knowledge of Krṣna.[48] Krṣna obliges with a comprehensive and detailed poetic description of his attributes but still Arjuna wants more and implores Krṣna: "I desire to see your supreme form, greatest of persons."[49] Krṣna then granted Arjuna divine vision to behold him: "Now see here in my body the entire universe of moving and unmoving things, and whatever else you desire to behold."[50] The *Gītā* describes what Arjuna saw:

> If the light of a thousand suns should all at once rise into the sky, that might approach the brilliance of that great person. Arjuna saw the entire universe in its multiplicity gathered there as one in the body of the God of gods.[51]

Arjuna sees the infinite Krṣna swallow up the enemy armies and is overwhelmed with terror and bewilderment regarding Krṣna's identity and purpose. Arjuna asked: "Tell me, who are you? I need to understand you; I cannot discern your purpose."[52] Krṣna answered:

> I am time run on, destroyer of the universe, risen here to annihilate worlds. Regardless of you all these warriors gathered against you, shall cease to exist. Therefore kill the enemy; they have already been killed by me. Simply be the instrument.[53]

Still terrified, Arjuna asks Krṣna to resume his familiar human form. Krṣna obliges and speaks:

This form of mine, which you have seen, is very hard to see. Only by exclusive devotion, can I be seen as I really am, and entered into. The one who acts for me, who
makes me the highest goal, who is devoted to me, who has abandoned attachment,
who is without hatred for any being, comes to me.[54]

By the end of the *Gītā*, Arjuna's doubts are dispelled and his courage is
restored: "My delusion has been obliterated, and through your grace I stand
and will do what you say."[55]

Between Kṛṣṇa and Jesus

The first person to translate the *Bhagavad Gītā* into English was so struck
with its similarity to the *Gospels* that he thought it borrowed its theme from
the *New Testament*.[56] Both Kṛṣṇa and Jesus claimed divine identity and
called disciples to exclusive devotion. They compared their relationship
with devotees to an intimate love relationship. Kṛṣṇa is the divine lover;
Jesus loves the church as his bride. Kṛṣṇa charges his devotees to act for the
welfare of the whole world just as Jesus calls his disciples to demonstrate
love to the world by loving each other. Kṛṣṇa and Jesus both call their followers to transcend self-interest through selfless devotion to God in service
to others.

Kṛṣṇa and Jesus see sacrifice as the meaning and purpose of life. Kṛṣṇa
identifies himself as the *Vedic* sacrifice that cyclically creates, sustains and
destroys the world while Jesus sees himself as the sacrificial lamb of God who
takes away the sins of the world. Jesus sacrificed himself to reconcile the world
to God and calls his followers to self-sacrificial service for the sake of others.
Kṛṣṇa exemplifies and teaches heroic sacrificial service for the sake of humanity. Both defend their respective kingdoms and defeat demonic forces of evil,
Kṛṣṇa by killing and Jesus by dying.

What Christians Might Learn From Kṛṣṇa

From Kṛṣṇa, Christians can learn the true nature of loving devotion in which
both actions and their results are offered exclusively to God without expecting anything in return, including reward or recognition. Kṛṣṇa teaches that all
actions should express sacrificial service to God and not be driven by ambition
to achieve a reward. True devotion is altruistic; it has no ulterior motive.

What Kṛṣṇa taught as the most sacred secret to those who are prepared to see it, Jesus hid in a parable for those who have ears to hear it:

> Suppose one of you has a servant plowing or looking after the sheep. Will he say to the servant when he comes in from the field, "Come along now and sit down to eat?" Won't he rather say, "Prepare my supper, get yourself ready and wait on me while I eat and drink; after that you may eat and drink?" Will he thank the servant because he did what he was told to do? No; so you also, when you have done everything you were told to do, should say, "We are unworthy servants; we have only done our duty."[57]

Notes

1. *Bhagavad Gītā* 4:8, Johnson, W. J., *The Bhagavad Gītā*, translated with an Introduction and Notes, Oxford University Press, 1994. All references to the *Bhagavad Gītā* are from this translation unless otherwise noted.
2. Singer, Milton, with Foreword by Daniel H. H. Ingalls, *Kṛṣṇa, in Myths, Rites and Attitudes*, University of Chicago Press, 1966.
3. *Bhagavad Gītā* 9:23–24.
4. *Rig Veda* 10:90, *The Rig Veda*, translated by Wendy Doniger, Penguin Books, 1981.
5. *Bhagavad Gītā* 4:13.
6. Malinar, Angelika, *The Bhagavadgītā: Doctrines and Disciplines*, Cambridge University Press, 2007.
7. *Bhāgavata Purāṇa*, Book 9, Chapter 24:66–67, *The Bhāgavata Purāṇa: Selected Readings*, Ravi M. Gupta and Kenneth R. Valpey, Columbia University Press, 2017.
8. *Bhāgavata Purāṇa* Book 10, Chapter 1. *Kṛṣṇa: The Beautiful Legend of God* (*Srimad Bhāgavata Purāṇa*), translated with an Introduction and Notes by Edwin F. Bryant, Penguin Books, 2003. All references to the *Bhāgavata Purāṇa* are based on this translation unless otherwise noted.
9. *Bhāgavata Purāṇa* 10:6.
10. *Bhāgavata Purāṇa* 10:7.
11. *Bhāgavata Purāṇa* 10:2.
12. *Bhāgavata Purāṇa* 10:24.
13. *Bhāgavata Purāṇa* 10:25.
14. *Bhāgavata Purāṇa* 10:20.
15. *Bhagavad Gītā* 9:32.
16. *Bhāgavata Purāṇa* 10:11.
17. *Bhāgavata Purāṇa* 10:11.
18. *Bhāgavata Purāṇa* 10:12.
19. *Bhāgavata Purāṇa* 10:15.
20. *Bhāgavata Purāṇa* 10:37.
21. *Bhāgavata Purāṇa* 10:16.
22. *Bhāgavata Purāṇa* 10:44.

23. *Bhāgavata Purāṇa* 11:1.
24. *Bhagavad Gītā* 1:26–27.
25. *Bhagavad Gītā* 1:39.
26. *Bhagavad Gītā* 1:45.
27. *Bhagavad Gītā* 1:46.
28. *Bhagavad Gītā* 1:26–46.
29. *Bhagavad Gītā* 2:3.
30. *Bhagavad Gītā* 2:4.
31. *Bhagavad Gītā* 2:11–13.
32. *Bhagavad Gītā* 2:19–22.
33. *Bhagavad Gītā* 2:31.
34. *Bhagavad Gītā* 2:38.
35. *Bhagavad Gītā* 2:37.
36. *Bhagavad Gītā* 2:47.
37. *Bhagavad Gītā* 2:61.
38. *Bhagavad Gītā* 3:1.
39. *Bhagavad Gītā* 3:19–20.
40. *Bhagavad Gītā* 6:1, 4.
41. *Bhagavad Gītā* 6:29–30.
42. *Bhagavad Gītā* 6:33–35.
43. *Bhagavad Gītā* 7:1–2.
44. *Bhagavad Gītā* 7:5–7, 13–14, 25.
45. *Bhagavad Gītā* 8:14, 16.
46. *Bhagavad Gītā* 9:34.
47. *Bhagavad Gītā* 10:7–8, 10–11.
48. *Bhagavad Gītā* 10:14, 16–17.
49. *Bhagavad Gītā* 11:3.
50. *Bhagavad Gītā* 11:7–8.
51. *Bhagavad Gītā* 11:12–13.
52. *Bhagavad Gītā* 11:31.
53. *Bhagavad Gītā* 11:32–33.
54. *Bhagavad Gītā* 11:52, 54–55.
55. *Bhagavad Gītā* 18:73.
56. Wilkins, Charles, *The Bhagvad-Geeta or Dialogues of Kreeshna and Arjoon*, translated from the original Sanskrit, British East India Company, 1785.
57. *Luke* 17:7–10, *Holy Bible: New International Version*, Zondervan Publishers, 1984.

· 4 ·

CONFUCIUS

Introduction

Confucius is China's premier teacher. Nearly every author who writes about Confucius discusses whether his teachings are a religion or a political philosophy; actually they were both. Confucius produced a form of humanism which, unlike the Greek ideal, made Heaven (*Tian*), not humanity, the measure of all things. Confucius had a deep sense of loyalty to Heaven, from which he believed he had received a mission to reform the world. His view of Heaven profoundly influenced his self-understanding and sense of identity: "No one understands me! I bear no grudge against Heaven nor do I blame others. I apply myself to learning in order to accomplish great things. Perhaps it is only Heaven that can understand me."[1]

His sayings were among the first that elementary school students learned to read and his teaching provided the standard curriculum for the education of those preparing for government service. His canon of classical literature continued to comprise the core of China's educational curriculum for over two millennia until the 20th-century Communist cultural revolution transformed China into a global industrial power. Nevertheless his ideas and values have been so deeply ingrained in the Chinese mind for so long that even today the impact of his character is indelible.

Socio-political Context

Confucius inherited a comprehensive socio-religious view of the world. The Chinese Classical texts revealed to Confucius a ritualized understanding of life on earth as it is in Heaven. Kings and commoners alike believed that human survival and success depended on harmony with the forces of Heaven. Heaven (*Tian*) was not a transcendent or remote realm but an immanent environment, an ever-expansive vaulted canopy of sky surrounding the earth and playing host, not only to stars and planets, but also to a hierarchy of spirits, including revered ancestors, natural forces and the deities that controlled them. People believed that their recently deceased relatives and ancient ancestors continued in life after death and were accessible through reciprocal ritual relationships with their living descendants. The deceased ancestors received food offerings and reverence to sustain and satisfy them; the ancestors in turn watched over the living and intervened to influence the course and quality of their lives.

More than a place, Heaven was thought of as an impersonal force and source of natural and moral order. Kings saw themselves as agents of Heaven who exercised authority on its behalf. They performed ritual sacrifices and ceremonies to ensure cosmic harmony between the forces of Heaven and the people of earth. The idea that political authority is derived from Heaven provided a firm ethical foundation for Chinese political philosophies.

For most of the first millennium before Christ, China was ruled by a single dynasty whose emperor was regarded as the Son of Heaven and ruled by the Mandate of Heaven (*Tian-ming*). As long as the ruler acted virtuously in accordance with Heaven, prosperity and peace were preserved—but emperors who failed to rule in harmony with the principles of Heaven lost the right to reign and were overthrown by the people. The ancient Chinese adage: "Heaven sees as its people see," is a seminal expression of democracy, the rule of the people.[2] Though the idea never developed into democracy in China, it served as the basis to hold emperors accountable to the higher power and principles of Heaven. Revolts and civil wars were justified by an appeal to the Mandate of Heaven.

Since the collapse of the Shang dynasty around the beginning of the first millennium BCE, rival feudal lords vied for control over a divided kingdom. The Zhou dynasty (1122–256 BCE) gradually conquered and controlled about 150 cities and villages, each ruled by a vassal king who served under the sovereignty of the Zhou emperor. The founders of the Zhou dynasty claimed that Heaven had ordained them to replace the Shang rulers who had become corrupt and consequently no longer preserved prosperity or peace among the people.

Zhou feudalism functioned effectively for the first three centuries of their dynastic rule, but in the eighth-century BCE, the assassination of the Zhou king left the empire with no central authority. Confucius lived during the "Spring and Autumn" period (770–476 BCE) of the Zhou dynasty, which was characterized by a fractured feudal system of independent domains clashing with each other for supremacy and survival. It was a chaotic period of political fragmentation and social unrest. The urgent concern of Confucius' generation was the same crisis that faces the world today: How can we learn to live in peace and harmony with each other?

In response to the common concern to restore political peace and reestablish social harmony, there arose a class of philosopher-advisors who attempted to discern the causes of disharmony and to discover how to save society. There were so many rival schools of thought that sixth century China came to be known as the age of the 100 philosophers. Philosophers like Confucius arose from a class of citizens who aspired to serve as soldiers, administrators or advisors to the state rulers. While state rulers fought each other for the right to unite and govern the warring states, philosophers competed with each other to influence and serve the state's leaders.

Confucius believed the answer to how we can live in peace and harmony with each other was preserved in the chronicles of Chinese history. He regarded the early Zhou period as a golden age of Chinese civilization, characterized by political peace, social stability, wise governing and high cultural achievements. He believed the people who best exemplified the ideal governing character were the ancient sage kings, especially the Duke of Zhou (1042–1030 BCE); the Duke ruled as regent after the death of his brother, King Wu, who was the founder and consolidator of the Zhou dynasty and an ancestor of the family that ruled over Confucius' home state.

The Duke of Zhou was praised as a selfless public servant who unified the recently established dynasty and successfully promoted economic prosperity and political peace. A perfect embodiment and model of humility, the Duke of Zhou relinquished his regency when his nephew, King Wu's son, reached the appropriate age to ascend his late father's throne. Confucius idolized the Duke of Zhou and declared himself a follower of the way of the Zhou.[3]

Texts as Context

For over two millennia, the Chinese civil service examination was primarily based on the Five Canonical Classics, which form the foundational Confucian canon of authoritative literature.[4] Tradition claims that Confucius compiled and edited these texts during the final years of his life but text-historical scholarship reveals that they were composed and compiled over several centuries before, during and after his life.

The first of these classics was the *Book of Odes*, a collection of folk songs and poetry which disclose details about the daily life of ordinary people prior to the birth of Confucius. The second text, the *Book of Documents*, contains official government records, conversations, and proclamations issued by kings and ruling nobility. The third, the *Spring and Autumn Annals*, was named for the historical period that it chronicles, and presents a chronological outline of important political events which focus on the royal activities in Confucius' home state of Lu. It provided principles of precedent for courts of law and government policy making, and the personalities presented in the texts are featured as role models for aspiring rulers to emulate. The fourth, the *Book of Change (I-jing)* is a manual for divination, the ancient art of discerning the will of Heaven by throwing stalks of straw and interpreting their patterns in light of corresponding cryptic commentary cataloged in the text. The fifth text, the *Book of Rituals*, is a collection of three small texts which provide details about ceremonies, rituals, rules of conduct, governmental structures and institutions.

According to traditional accounts, soon after his death, the surviving disciples of Confucius convened to carefully record from memory his sayings and conversations in a collection of nearly 500 aphorisms arranged in 20 chapters now known as the *Analects (Lunyu)*. Text historical analysis reveals that while it accurately presents the dialogues and sayings of Confucius, it also contains additional comments which were periodically edited into the original text until reaching its final form sometime in the middle of the third century BCE. It is a practical guidebook for constructing a harmonious, hierarchical society through cultural education and exemplary ethical leadership. Its central theme concerns the perfection of human conduct and character, which is to be cultivated within the context of well-defined interpersonal social relationships. The *Analects* are the primary source for the life and teachings of Confucius.

Birth and Youth

Confucius was born about five and a half centuries before Christ in the town of Zou in the small state of Lu in Northern China during the Zhou dynasty in politically turbulent times. His family traced its lineage all the way back to the royal house of the Shang and his ancestors were aristocrats. However, when Confucius' great grandfather lost the prestige and privilege of political power, the Kong family fell on hard times. Confucius, the younger son of his father's concubine, was born and raised in relative poverty. His father, Kong He, was a dignified soldier who died in battle when Confucius was only three. Standing six feet, eight inches tall, Confucius' father was a giant of a man from whom Confucius inherited his towering stature. His father had nine daughters and a disabled son, but longed for a son who could properly perform the family's ancestral ceremonies. Desperate for an eligible heir, Kong He took a young woman from the family of Yan who bore a healthy son and named him Kong Qui, which, ever since its mispronunciation by 17th-century Jesuit missionaries, has been known as Confucius. He was raised by a single mother who instilled in him a deep sense of compassion and concern for people.

The only able-bodied son of his widowed mother, Confucius learned early to labor in love to support her, a crippled elder brother, and two younger sisters. As a menial worker, Confucius identified with the concerns of common laborers. Hard work shaped his deep sense of dignity and humility. Later in life, Confucius told his disciples: "When I was young, I was in humble circumstances; for this reason, I acquired some simple skills in several pursuits."[5]

As a boy Confucius enjoyed fishing, though not with a net, and archery, though he never shot at sitting ducks, only at birds in flight.[6] In childhood, he played with ritual vessels and utensils, pretending to conduct royal rites and perform official government ceremonies.

Childhood Education

In ancient China, aristocratic boys began education around age seven. Because his family could not afford private instruction, Confucius taught himself by reading literature produced in a prior golden age of Chinese history. "I was not born with the knowledge that I have: I just like to study the ancients, and I pursue their ideas with diligence."[7] "By age 15, I set my mind on learning."[8] Confucius saw himself as a great lover of learning. "In a town of ten thousand households, there must certainly be those as loyal and trustworthy as I, but none who cares as much about learning as I do."[9] He was a conscientious student: "When studying, it seems like there's not enough time, and once something is learned, there's always the fear of losing it."[10] Learning for Confucius had a practical aim: "Isn't it a pleasure to study and then put into practice what you learn?"[11] He was open to learning from anyone:

> If there are three people walking along, there will be one I can learn from. I notice their strong points and work to emulate them; I also notice their defects and try to change if I see them in myself as well.[12]

Marriage and Early Career

His first position was in public service, as he was appointed overseer of a granary for his home district. After a successful year, he was promoted to manager of grazing and grounds. Tradition tells us that the cattle and sheep were properly fattened under his management.

At age 19 Confucius married a woman from the Qiguan family. A year later she bore a son named Kong Li and eventually a daughter who would later marry one of Confucius' disciples. Four years later around age 23, Confucius abandoned public service to mourn the death of his mother. For the traditional three-year mourning period, he refrained from sensual indulgences and social entertainments; instead he devoted himself to the study of the ancient art of government.

Scholar-Teacher

At the end of the three-year mourning period, he became a teacher and attracted young men who were ambitious to serve in government. Confucius wanted to restore peace and order and studied rituals and legends in old books to discover guidelines for the present day. He believed that justice, honesty, and concern for common people were the principles of Heaven that kings and rulers needed to guide the government for the benefit of the population. When Confucius was 34 years old, an influential government official recommended to the king that Confucius be sent to the Zhou capital city to study the ceremonies. It was in these ancient royal rituals that Confucius discovered the hidden wisdom by which rulers conducted government in harmony with Heaven, and by which ordinary people could regulate their lives and cultivate their characters.

A philosopher of education, he established and fulfilled the prerequisite for teaching: "If you are well-versed in the ancient and understand the modern, you may become a teacher of others."[13] He relished in his role as scholar-teacher: "To quietly recite and memorize the Classics, to love learning without tiring of it, to never be bored with teaching, how could these be difficult for me?"[14] Education was not merely a means to an end—it was the meaning of life itself. For Confucius, education was not mindless memorization of dates and details; its aim was nothing less than the perfection of moral character and the total reformation of society. "Learning without thinking is labor lost; thinking without learning is perilous."[15] He expected and required much from his students:

> If a student doesn't feel troubled in his studies, I don't enlighten him. If a student doesn't get frustrated in his studies, I don't explain to him; if I point out one corner and he cannot point out the other three, I don't repeat myself.[16]

He taught practical knowledge about the art of governing, which he learned from his study of the ancient rulers. A veritable one-man university, he also taught archery, history, mathematics, music, ethics, ritual, dance and poetry. The purpose of education is the perfection of personal character, which is also the foundation of an ideal society.

Unlike other private tutors who only served aristocrats, he offered instruction to anyone who sincerely wanted to learn how to serve the government regardless of their social status or ability to pay tuition. "For anyone who brings even a small token of appreciation, I have yet to refuse instruction."[17] In this way he became China's first public school teacher. "In education there are no class distinctions."[18] Confucius believed that education was crucial for personal character development. "By nature, people are pretty much alike; it is learning and practice that set them apart."[19]

His disciples candidly recalled his character and personality as a teacher: "Confucius was gentle yet firm, dignified but not harsh, respectful, yet well at ease."[20] They also tell us: "When he was pleased with someone's singing, he would ask them to repeat the song so he could sing along."[21] Another student described his disposition and demeanor: "The master is congenial, pleasant, courteous and good-tempered. In this way he engages the world different from other people."[22]

He instilled in his students a love of learning: "To realize by the day all the things you don't know, and not to forget by the month what you have mastered, this can be called love of learning."[23] Confucius established a criteria for true understanding with the answer to a rhetorical question he posed to one of his students: "Zhong Yu, do you understand what I have taught you? To understand and say you understand, or to not understand and say you don't understand—that's true understanding."[24]

Government Servant

At age 50, Confucius entered government service as the chief magistrate of a local municipality. Later he was promoted to minister of justice serving in the capacity of police commissioner. According to tradition, while he was the minister of justice, people could keep their doors unlocked. And if anyone dropped a valuable on the street, it would be picked up by a passerby and promptly returned. Despite a modicum of success in government, political jealousies and rivalries forced Confucius to resign from office in disgust but not despair.

Mission and Message

Disenfranchised and alienated, Confucius gathered together a few of his favorite disciples and began a 14-year trek, traveling by foot throughout the many divided dynastic districts in search of a ruler who would listen to his ideas and strategies to restore China to its former glory. Given the chance, he believed he could change the world. "Were any prince to employ me, even in a single year a good deal could be done, and in three years everything could be accomplished."[25]

During his missionary journey, he solicited and secured the audience of a few rulers, but to no avail. He spoke truth to power and paid the price of persecution for it. He was candidly critical of contemporary rulers. For example, when one local magistrate attempted to court favor with Confucius by feigning to seek his advice on how best to govern his state, "Confucius said: why ask me about governing your state when you have not yet learned how to govern yourself?" He was mocked and ridiculed by the very politicians he tried to persuade with his message. When an assassination attempt was made on his life, he responded: "Heaven has empowered me with virtue, what can a mere man do to me?"[26]

Throughout his life Confucius pursued three inseparable goals: to serve government, to teach youth, and to transmit the ideals of ancient Chinese culture to posterity. He was a man with a mission. Confucius proposed a comprehensive program to transform society in the image of the ancients. He reintroduced and reinterpreted ideas and institutions of the past for the sake of the future. "I am a transmitter and not an innovator. I believe in and have a passion for the ancients."[27]

Death and Legacy

After the 14-year trek with his disciples throughout China, Confucius returned to his native state of Lu where he spent his final days teaching, compiling and editing the Classical texts that served as the source of his wisdom.

As Confucius approached age 70, his only son died, and a year later, his favorite disciple Yen Yuan also died. Confucius cried out in despair: "Heaven has forsaken me; Heaven has forsaken me."[28] Soon thereafter, in great grief, Confucius himself passed away at the age of 73. Because his highest ambition lay in politics, he died perhaps thinking himself a failure; fortunately his disciples did not disappoint. After his death, half of his students managed to procure important, influential government posts through which they effectively implemented Confucian principles and practices.

Summary

In a single pithy passage, Confucius conveyed a chronological outline of his autobiography:

> At fifteen I was intent on study, at thirty I had established myself, at forty I had no uncertainty, at fifty I knew the Mandate of Heaven, at sixty I was in constant harmony with things, and at seventy I could follow my heart's desire without overstepping convention.[29]

Teachings

Culture of Courtesies (*Li*)

Confucius proposed a ritualization of activities and relationships as the spiritual solution to a socio-political problem. The principle Chinese cultural value to which Confucius appealed is *Li*. It is the controlling concept that provides the context for the practice of a comprehensive Confucian culture of courtesies. The term *Li* is multivalent, encompassing a wide range of meanings such as ritual, custom, manners, etiquette, propriety and decorum. *Li* is the means for ordering life and establishing harmony. A person regulated by *Li* is virtuous and spiritually aligned with the Way of Heaven; a state governed by *Li* is peaceful and prosperous. *Li* perfectly reflected the cosmic order, and socio-spiritual harmony was the inevitable result of acting appropriately in accord with the Way of Heaven.

The ancient meaning of *Li* referred to hospitality rituals performed to revere, placate and petition deities and deceased ancestors who were in a position to influence the living for better or worse. In this original sense, *Li* was synonymous with what is now meant by the term religion. Confucius transformed a concept, which applied specifically to the reverence of ancestors and deities, into a ritualization of all social interaction and activities. *Li* infused a solemn sense of spirituality and mystery into ordinary daily life in the world.

For Confucius, every interpersonal relationship is scripted. People are not left on their own to innovate, improvise or invent ways to behave toward elders, equals, superiors or siblings. There is a cultural protocol of courteous customs designed to define, regulate and facilitate each family and social relationship. A code of courteous conduct specific to each relationship ensures that people always know how to play their respective roles in the ceremony of life.

For Confucius, spirituality is experienced in and through personal relationships. All forms of Confucian culture are permeated with the didactic purpose of promoting values that help perfect the practice of everyday personal relationships. All kinds of cultural arts—toys, theatre, song, dance, poetry, parades and pageants—are calculated to cultivate virtuous character in all citizens. Confucius said: "Personal cultivation begins with poetry, is made firm by rules of decorum, and is perfected by music."[30]

The Root of All Relationships (*Ren*)

All cultural arts are intended to inspire and instill the ideal of human-heartedness (*Ren*). Confucius rooted every relationship in a single central virtue called *Ren*. The original Chinese pictogram for this foundational value depicts a person and the number two; it signifies the ideal relationship between any two people. It has been variously translated as benevolence, human-heartedness, love, empathy and altruism. To embody *Ren* is the aim of human life in the world.

Ren is the human character quality acquired by the practice of *Li*; human-heartedness is cultivated by internalizing the reverence and respect reflected in proper ritual performance that is not merely mechanical but moral and meaningful. *Ren* is the measure of personal character and the goal of self-cultivation; it is the personal attitude and effort reflected in the performance of *Li*. Confucius said: "If a person lacks *Ren* what does such a one have to do with *Li*?"[31] Self-cultivation means self-control. Confucius said: "To master the self and return to *Li*, that is *Ren*."[32] *Ren* and *Li* are two sides of the same coin. When asked, what is *Ren*, Confucius said:

> *Ren* is overcoming one's selfish desires and acting in accordance with propriety (*Li*). It comes from oneself; it is not something others can give you. And how specifically is one to act in accordance with benevolence (*Ren*)? If it is contrary to propriety (*Li*), don't listen to it, don't say it, don't do it.[33]

While Heaven is an impersonal source and force of moral principle, its virtues are revealed and embodied in interpersonal social interaction modeled on family relationships. "Confucius said: If a person sets his mind on benevolence (*Ren*), he will do no evil."[34]

Five Foundational Relationships

Ren is the basis of all relationships and the root of *Ren* is filial piety.

> Confucius student Yu Ruo asked about filial virtue. Confucius said: Nowadays what people mean by filial piety is merely providing for one's parents; but dogs and horses are also provided for. Without feeling deep respect for one's parents, what's the difference?[35]

Confucius had a utopian vision for world peace and harmony. His philosophy is rooted in family values that overflow into compassionate concern for humanity. It all begins with the relationship between a parent and child. The cornerstone value is filial piety, which means reverential respect and devoted love that flows from children to parents.

> There are few people who, being thoughtful toward their parents and older siblings, would then offend a superior out in society. And it is unheard of for someone who wouldn't offend a superior to cause trouble elsewhere in society. An ideal person concentrates on the root and when the root is firmly established, the Way of Heaven springs forth. Being thoughtful toward one's parents and older siblings is the root of benevolent action.[36]

Parents inspire their children to internalize filial piety by instilling them with love and guidance. The parent-child relationship is the most important of all interpersonal relationships because it also provides the paradigm for the relationship between the ruler and citizens. A ruler, like a parent, should be benevolent while citizens should be devoted and loyal. Spouses should love and listen to each other attentively. Since Confucius was the product of a patriarchal society, he upheld traditional patterns of hierarchical authority in which wives heeded husbands who reciprocated with compassion and concern. Elder siblings are to provide guidance and a good example to younger siblings who, for their part, are to be respectful and deferential. Friendships outside the family are modeled on relationships within it.

The five fundamental relationships are the foundation of a harmonious and peaceful society. Simply stated, if each person learns to play their proper role within the basic family unit, and if those roles are properly extended beyond the family to include all interpersonal social relationships, then the whole society can operate harmoniously with peace and love prevailing.

The Power of Moral Example (*De*)

While the cultivation of character begins in the family, Confucius felt it was the moral responsibility of government rulers and officials to set the ethical example for others to emulate. The ideal king embodies *Ren* and rules by *Li*. "Confucius said: if a ruler can administer the state with decorum and courtesy, then what difficulty will he have?"[37]

The source of a successful king's power is virtue (*De*). Confucius believed that virtue was contagious and could be caught, like the common cold, by association with those who possess it. Confucius idolized the ideal scholar-administrator Duke of Zhou because he embodied *De* in his character and his very presence in the world radiated peace and ensured socio-political harmony between Heaven and earth.

> When asked about government, Confucius said: To govern is to set things right. If you begin by setting yourself right, who will dare to deviate from the right?[38] If a ruler is upright, all will go well without orders. But if he is not upright, even though he gives orders, they won't be obeyed.[39]

He believed the power of moral example is far more effective than political pressure or punitive measures. He strongly disagreed with those who felt that order in society could only be restored by a government administering strict laws and levying severe penalties for violations.

> Lead them by means of laws and keep order among them by punishments, and people will learn to avoid getting caught but will lack any sense of shame. Lead them through moral force and keep order among them through rituals and they will have a sense of shame and will also correct themselves.[40]

When asked about the proper way to govern, "Confucius said: Put others first and give credit where credit is due. What else? Do these two things tirelessly."[41] When asked about governmental use of capital punishment, Confucius replied:

> In administering your government, what is the need to kill? Desire the good yourself and the people will be good. The virtue of the leaders is like the wind and the people are like the grass. Let the wind blow and the grass is sure to bend.[42]

Virtue (De) distinguished sage-kings above ordinary people and Confucius used their example to inspire and popularize proper conduct. Confucius taught his students that the source of all virtue (De) is Heaven and it can be found in and through study: "Studying extensively, maintaining firm determination, questioning sincerely and reflecting on things at hand, benevolence is found in the midst of these."[43] Character development requires studying, learning and following the way of the ancient sages.

Between Confucius and Jesus

Confucius and Jesus were clearly kindred spirits. Both were radical re-interpreters of the traditions they inherited. They were champions of truth, justice and compassion. Confucius, like Jesus, spoke truth to power. The golden rule of Jesus echoes the saying of Confucius: "Don't do to others what you don't want them to do to you."[44] Confucius and Jesus not only invested themselves in the lives of their disciples, but also depended on them for the fulfillment of their missions. Both were itinerant teachers with a vision to transform the world though their visions of Heaven and earth are worlds apart.

For Confucius, Heaven is a universal moral force, and on earth human rulers are to govern in harmony with it. The will of Heaven is reflected in harmonious human relations. If people conduct themselves in accordance with the way of Heaven, peace and justice will prevail on earth. Confucius had confidence in the capacity of common people to cultivate their characters into an ideal image of humanity. Spirituality is experienced between people in properly polite and caring, reciprocal relationships.

Heaven is a power to which people pray and the source of moral principles to which people are to conform; however, Heaven is not a person with whom one might experience a relationship. While Confucius locates the origin of compassion and morality in Heaven, he believes that humanity has the innate ability and divine mandate to manifest the way of Heaven on earth. "Confucius said: It is people that can make the way of Heaven great, not the way of Heaven that can make people great."[45]

Unlike Confucius, Jesus did not seek or desire government office nor did he see human government as the way to achieve justice, peace and harmony in the world. Jesus placed no confidence in human nature. When the Roman governor, Pilate, asked Jesus to clarify his claim to be king of the Jews, Jesus declared clearly: "My kingdom is not of this world."[46] For Jesus, the kingdom of God is a quality of life in relationship with God; it is a community of people in covenantal relationship with God and each other through a common commitment to Jesus.

For Confucius, Heaven and earth are complementary halves of a unified and harmonious whole. At its best earth may mirror Heaven. However for Jesus, the kingdom of God and the kingdoms of earth are two rival realms of reality governed and guided by radically different sources. Satan tempted Jesus with the kingdoms of the world and all its glory but Jesus refused the offer. The kingdom of God is not accomplished by human achievement, political power, military might or social engineering. The gospel first and foremost announces the arrival of the kingdom of God on earth; it descends from above, from a higher order.

For Jesus, the kingdom of God is at odds with the kingdoms and rulers of this world. The kingdom that Jesus preached is radically different from the way human nature operates and orders society. The kingdom of God subverts common core cultural values; it supplants the hierarchical harmony of humanity. In the kingdom of God, the last will be first and the first will be last.[47]

The kingdom of God is not built on human wisdom or human principles but on the nature and character of God revealed in Jesus. A new era has arrived with the coming of the *Messianic* king. It is not a romantic return to a mythical, glorious, golden past, nor is it a new age of political peace and prosperity; instead it is an extended period of personal and communal growth and development during which disciples of Jesus bear fruit for the kingdom of God. Yet the kingdom of God grows alongside the kingdoms of earth.[48] The two kingdoms are parallel but incompatible and irreconcilable realms of reality. Jesus calls his disciples to align themselves with the kingdom of God, to store treasures in heaven and not on earth, and to pray and hope for the kingdom to come as completely on earth as it is in heaven.

What Christians Might Learn From Confucius

Family Values

Christians can learn from Confucius to focus on family roles, relationships and responsibilities. Family relationships are crucial in the formation and development of moral character. The Christian family is a crucible in which characters are forged and fashioned into the image of Jesus.

Some texts appear to portray Jesus as anti-family and anti-social, but nothing could be farther from the truth. Jesus did say: "If anyone comes to me and does not hate father and mother, wife and children, brothers and sisters, yes, even their own life, such a person cannot be my disciple."[49] But those words, if taken out of context, can be misleading. Matthew recalls the same words of Jesus which clarify the meaning: "Anyone who loves father or mother more than me is not worthy of me and anyone who loves their son or daughter more than me is not worthy of me."[50] It is a matter of primary loyalty. In Jesus' day and throughout history, persecution of Christians involves the betrayal of family members. Following Jesus entails taking sides, even if it means being forsaken by family.

Nevertheless, it is within the family that we learn to respect authority. Family relationships shape our basic understanding of love and form our foundational sense of justice and empathy. Jesus was born into a family of parents and siblings. He learned love and life values, like everybody else, at his mother's breast, on his father's knee, and at the side of his brothers and sisters.

Jesus did not generally call people to abandon their families. He affirmed marriage by performing his first public miracle at a wedding, and he demonstrated committed concern for his mother even in his final words. While he hung dying on the cross, Jesus saw his mother and favorite disciple standing nearby and addressed them both: "Woman, here is your son, and to his disciple he said: Here is your mother. From that time on the disciple took her into his home."[51] And while Jesus was never a father or spouse, he was certainly a son and a brother. He was first and foremost a family man and understood his own identity as the Son of his heavenly father.

It is within the family that siblings learn to assume responsibility for themselves and each other. "Am I my brother's keeper?"[52] Jesus and Confucius concur; the answer is yes, you are. Self-sacrificial love is discovered, experienced and expressed in marriage and the family. The utopian vision of Confucius is rooted in the family, and Jesus expands and extends his family to include: "Whoever does the will of my father in heaven is my brother and sister and mother."[53]

Notes

1. *Analects* 14:35, *The Sayings of Confucius: The Teachings of China's Greatest Sage*, translated by James Ware, Mentor Books, 1955. All references to the Analects are from this translation unless otherwise noted.

2. *Mencius* 17 *The Works of Mencius*, translated with critical and exegetical notes, prolegomena, and copious indexes by James Legge, Clarendon Press, Oxford, 1895.

3. *Analects* 3:14.

4. Five Classics include the *Books of Odes, Book of Documents, Spring and Autumn Annals, Book of Change, Book of Rites*; and the Four Books are the *Doctrine of the Mean, Great Learning, Mencius* and *Analects*.

5. *Analects* 9:6.

6. *Analects* 7:26.

7. *Analects* 7:20.

8. *Analects* 2:4.

9. *Analects* 5:27.

10. *Analects* 8:17.

11. *Analects* 1:1.

12. *Analects* 7:22.

13. *Analects* 2:11.

14. *Analects* 7:2.

15. *Analects* 2:15.
16. *Analects* 7:8.
17. *Analects* 7:7.
18. *Analects* 15:38–39.
19. *Analects* 17:2.
20. *Analects* 7:37.
21. *Analects* 7:31.
22. *Analects* 10:2.
23. *Analects* 19:5.
24. Analects 2:17.
25. *Analects* 13:10.
26. *Analects* 7:22.
27. *Analects* 7:1.
28. *Analects* 11:8.
29. *Analects* 2:4.
30. *Analects* 8:8.
31. *Analects* 3:3.
32. *Analects* 12:1.
33. *Analects* 12:1.
34. *Analects* 4:4.
35. *Analects* 2:7.
36. *Analects* 1:2.
37. *Analects* 4:13.
38. *Analects* 12:17.
39. *Analects* 13:6.
40. *Analects* 2:3.
41. *Analects* 13:1.
42. *Analects* 12:19.
43. *Analects* 19:6.
44. *Analects* 12:2; 15:24.
45. *Analects* 15:28.
46. *John* 18:36, *Holy Bible: New International Version*, Zondervan Publishers, 1984. All references to the Bible are from this translation unless otherwise noted.
47. *Matthew* 20:16.
48. *Matthew* 13:24–30.
49. *Luke* 14:26.
50. *Matthew* 10:37.
51. *John* 19:26–27.
52. *Genesis* 4:9.
53. *Matthew* 12:5.

· 5 ·

LAOZI

Introduction

Daoism refers to a family of related religious and philosophical traditions which trace their roots to Laozi, the original title of the *Daodejing* and the name of its legendary author. The prehistoric beginnings of Daoism are shrouded in the mystery of Chinese antiquity. It has no single source of origin or first founder. It gradually emerged and evolved from several sources into a diversity of Chinese cultural beliefs and practices. Daoist inspired arts and sciences include martial arts like Tai Chi, Taekwondo and Karate. Traditional Chinese cuisine, medicine, architecture and astrology are among the many sciences based on Daoist views of the body as a microcosm of the universe. Everything from acupuncture to the zodiac has its roots in Daoist theories for which tradition recognizes Laozi among its legendary foundational figures.

Socio-political Context

Laozi inherited the same socio-political situation as Confucius (see Chapter Four). Although tradition locates Laozi in the sixth-century BCE, text historical scholars situate the text associated with him (*Daodejing*) three centuries later during the final phase of the Zhou dynasty known as the Warring States period (480–222 BCE). The fractured feudalism into which Confucius and Laozi were born had degenerated into a culture of constant interstate warfare by the time the *Daodejing* reached its final form. The Warring States period began about the time Confucius died. The many rival family-states vying for supremacy had been reduced to seven, four of whom continued to wage war until one of them, the Ch'in (221–206 BCE) from whom China derives its name, emerged triumphant as the first imperial empire to unify the lands of many feuding families under a single central authority.

The Zhou dynasty into which Laozi was born traced its ancestral roots back to the legendary Hou Ji, who taught them the science of seeds and agriculture. Throughout their history, socio-economic policy centered around land distribution and management, which favored the farmer over the merchant and artisan. Agriculture is production; commerce is merely exchange. Only rulers and scholars, who were usually land owners, enjoyed higher social status than the menial laborers who farmed their lands. Since scholars depended on produce from their property, their thoughts were never far from the concerns of farmers. Consequently, scholars were in close contact with nature and observed the movements of the sun and moon and the succession of seasons, noting favorable times for ploughing and planting. They were in touch with the earth and in tune with the rhythms of nature.

Laozi was representative of an emerging countercultural group of scholarly recluses who idolized the simplicity of farmers and primitive society while criticizing and condemning civilization. In Laozi's assessment, civilization is itself the source of hostile aggression on which societies depend for their competitive producers and fierce fighters. Cruelty wears the cloak of civility. Whereas Confucius looked to a past glorious age of political peace and perfection, Laozi longed for a return to an era before civilization created its own crisis of conflicts. Laozi expresses the aspirations and inspirations of the farmer and draws sharp distinctions between the natural ways of the universe and the artificial ways of civilized society. Whereas Confucius proposed the ritualization of all activity as the solution to social disharmony, Laozi recommended acting in harmony with nature as the best way to absorb and quell the hostile aggression on which competitive society is based and built. The *Daodejing* can be read as a radical reaction to the crisis of struggle for survival in a world full of hostile aggression. "Violent and fierce people don't die a natural death; I shall make this the father of my teaching."[1]

Texts as Context

The *Daodejing* is a repository of ancient wit and wisdom collected into a collage of 81 chapters which are conveyed succinctly in 5,000 words. It is a loose collection of sayings gathered from Laozi and other sages like him; it is not designed to persuade people by logic but to shock and shake them with the power of pithy poems and paradoxical prose. The first half of the collection concerns *Dao*, the Way, and the second half deals with its operational power, *De*.

The *Daodejing* has been translated more than any other book in the world with the single exception of the Bible. The text lends itself to multiple translations because its words are multivalent, ambiguous and suggestive of a plurality of meanings. Its brevity and archaic, aphoristic language also contribute to the difficulties in discerning exactly what the text says and means. Moreover, there are no dates, places, persons or historic events mentioned anywhere in the text that might help situate the *Daodejing* in its historical context.

Archaeologists unearthed bamboo slips from a Southern Chinese tomb in 1993 that included 31 chapters of the *Daodejing* dated to around 300 BCE; this discovery confirmed the ancient origins of the text, which is traditionally believed to originate during the sixth-century BCE. Previously in 1973, three graves which had been sealed since 168 BCE were excavated from a tomb in Honan; in addition to many artifacts two complete copies of the manuscript written on silk were discovered in the tomb.

These discoveries verify the accuracy and reliability with which the text was transmitted inter-generationally, though the oldest complete manuscript reverses the order of presentation, introducing first *De* and then *Dao*. The discoveries also support text-historical scholarship that suggests it was composed and compiled over several centuries until reaching its final form by the mid-second-century BCE, by which time it had already become important enough to be interred in a tomb. The standard edition of the text was established in the third-century of the common era and is the basis for most English translations.

Birth and Career

Legends surrounding the birth of Laozi are mythological but nevertheless instructive, dramatizing the auspicious nature of his origin. One fantastic story claims he was conceived in his mother's womb as she gazed upon a shooting star, a meteor descending from Heaven. More stupendously, the myth relates how his mother remained pregnant with him for 62 years before giving birth to the child already endowed with long white hair, a beard, wrinkled skin and the ability to speak. Immediately after being born, Laozi pointed to the plum tree against which his mother leaned to deliver him and declared: "I take my surname from this tree." *Li* means plum, to which he prefixed *Her*, which means ear, because his were unusually long; despite this initial name everybody called him Laozi which means old-master since he was born with white hair and a beard. While no one takes the legend literally, it reveals the importance which the Chinese attribute to the wisdom that comes only with age. In Chinese culture, respect flows from younger to older; age is honored because it is associated with wisdom. Laozi was reputed to embody the wisdom of the universe.

The old-master was born in the small village of Jen, in the county of Qu and the Kingdom of Chu located in Southern China. Beyond that we know next to nothing about his childhood or early years. In adulthood, he worked in the Chinese imperial capital at Loyang as a custodian of books and as an archivist of the Zhou emperor's official government documents. He was married and had a son named Zong who became a successful soldier. Laozi passed his days studying manuscripts containing the wisdom and ways of ancient China. Although he did not start a school of his own or recruit students, many were attracted to him and became disciples. He acquired a reputation for possessing great knowledge, and news about him reached the ears of Confucius.

According to an early Daoist source, Confucius traveled to meet with Laozi to discover the wisdom the librarian had learned. After several days under the tutelage of the old-master, Confucius respectfully thanked Laozi and requested permission to return home, but Laozi detained Confucius and gave him two more pieces of unsolicited advice before bidding him farewell. First, Laozi told Confucius that the ancient sages Confucius studied and taught were actually dead, their bones were rotting in their graves, and their surviving words should not be taken too seriously. Second, the best people in the world are simple; abandon your pride and ambition because they will not help you. Confucius returned home confounded but full of awe for Laozi. He reported about the meeting to his disciples:

> For animals that run there are traps, for birds that fly there are arrows, for fish that swim there are nets but who knows how the ungraspable, unfathomable dragon mounts the clouds and ascends to the sky? Today I have met a dragon; today I met Laozi.[2]

Renunciation and Disappearance

In the middle of his ordinary and uneventful career, Laozi became disillusioned and disgusted with the warring world in which he lived. In response to the same political and social upheaval that other philosophers faced, Laozi did not offer an alternative solution. He resigned his government post, climbed on the back of a water buffalo, and rode through the Han-ku pass which leads westward from Loyang to the border. There he was detained and interrogated by *Yinxi*, the gatekeeper who discerned that Laozi was a national treasure trove of wisdom, placed him under arrest, and compelled him to commit his knowledge to writing.

After two days and nights, Laozi emerged from solitary confinement with a collection of 81 cryptic poems known as the *Daodejing* (*The Classic of the Way and its Operation*). Upon relinquishing his hand-written manuscript to the border guard, Laozi re-mounted his water buffalo and rode off into the sunset, never to be seen or heard from again.[3]

Laozi had no intention whatsoever to establish religious traditions or philosophical schools, yet the 81 peculiar poems he produced in prison under pressure became the foundational text for a variety of religious traditions and philosophical interpretations. Laozi took no initiative to teach anything to anyone; he launched no mission and left no clear message. Nevertheless, the legacy of Laozi is preserved in a perplexing puzzle of profound poems concerning the way of the universe and its natural operation.

Teachings

The Way (*Dao*)

The word *Dao* had a long history of usage before Laozi. While the term simply means path, road or way, various rival Chinese philosophers disputed over its meaning; each argued for his own version and vision of how to access and apply the *Dao* to the problems of life in the world.[4] Confucius promoted the moral way of Heaven expressed in propriety but Laozi attuned himself to the *Dao* as the regulating principle of the universe revealed in the rhythmic way of nature.

Ineffable and Inconceivable. The very first words of the *Daodejing* introduce the *Dao* as unutterable, inexpressible and beyond all names and words. "The *Dao* that can be named is not the true *Dao*."[5] The basic motivating force in the universe is indescribable. So mysterious is the *Dao* that "those who know it, do not speak of it and those who speak of it, do not know it."[6] Laozi understood that ordinary people would ridicule his reasoning. "The common person, on hearing about true *Dao*, laughs loudly at it; had he not laughed, it would not be the true *Dao*."[7] *Dao* is beyond ordinary sense perceptions and normal ways of knowing. It cannot be grasped by logic, math or science. The body and mind are ill-equipped to comprehend it.

Creator and Sustainer. *Dao* is not a thing—it is that through which all things come to be. It is not a being, but the nonbeing through which the many different beings come to exist. Being and nonbeing are dual aspects of *Dao*.

> Nonbeing is the origin of Heaven and Earth; being is the mother of all things. There-fore let there always be nonbeing so we may see their subtlety and let there always be being so we may see their outcome. The two are the same but after they are produced, they have different names. They both may be called deep and profound. Deeper and more profound, the door of all subtleties.[8]

Dao not only brings things into being but also nurtures and sustains them.

> There is something undifferentiated and complete, which existed before Heaven and Earth. Soundless and formless, it depends on nothing and doesn't change. It operates everywhere and is free from danger. It may be considered the mother of the universe. I do not know its name; I call it *Dao*. If forced to give it a name, I shall call it great. Now being great means functioning everywhere.[9]

Laozi teaches that happiness is found in attaining mystical union with *Dao* through mind-emptying meditative methods.[10] *Dao* is the source of all change but does not itself change. It depicts ultimate reality as a perpetual process of dynamic interaction and adaptation guided by an indescribable principle that operates according to its own mysterious nature. From this Laozi deduced that the only way to be happy is to be in harmony with the source that creates and sustains everything.

For Laozi, the *Dao* is nonbeing—yet what it lacks is the very thing that makes it useful. Doorways, windows, cups and bowls are all missing something, but what they lack is the very thing that makes them useful. The empty space in a window and door makes it possible to see and pass through, and the empty part of the cup and bowl enables them to contain water and food.

Thirty spokes are united around a hub to make a wheel, but it is on its nonbeing that the utility of the wheel depends. Clay is molded to form a cup, but it is on its nonbeing that the utility of the cup depends. By adding and removing clay we form a vessel. By carving, doors and windows are cut out to make a room, but it is on its nonbeing that the utility of the room depends. Therefore turn being into advantage and nonbeing into utility.[11]

A *Theory of Relativity*. Prior to Laozi, Chinese philosophers explained the operation of the universe in terms of two opposite, yet complementary forces called *yin* and *yang*. Though opposite, the forces do not compete; instead they cooperate with each other to maintain balance and harmony in nature and throughout the universe. *Yin* is feminine, negative, dark, heavy, cool and passive; *yang* is masculine, positive, light, warm and aggressive. Nothing is completely one or the other; everything is a mixture of both. There is no *yin* without *yang*; they are interdependent forces that always interact with each other. They invade and inter-penetrate each other so that *yin* resides at the very center of *yang* and vice versa. Neither one is good or bad in itself but an excess of either one is bad while a balance of both is good.

Things develop in alternating movements of *yin* and *yang*. Everything is relative. Like polar magnetic forces, *yin* and *yang* interact by the law of nature—without lawgiver or judge. Laozi presented *Dao* as the source of *yin* and *yang* to account for their existence and to explain the dynamic interaction that occurs between them. *Dao* establishes the identity of opposites. It exposes opposites as two sides of the same coin. Being and nonbeing are enveloped by *Dao*. Nonbeing is the essence of the *Dao* and being is its operational power. This means that *Dao* encompasses both being and nonbeing. Opposites are differentiating developments of the same single reality. Paradox and polarity are inherent in everything. To achieve balance means to be free from opposites and remain undifferentiated and unified like a child. As people become civilized through the process of socialization, the sense of unity with *Dao* is lost and dualities dominate the mind. Laozi's goal is to return to the *Dao*. Only by forgetting and abandoning the mind and senses can a person directly intuit the *Dao* and attune to the rhythm and movement of mother nature.

Being and nonbeing produce each other; difficult and easy complete each other; long and short contrast each other; high and low distinguish each other; sound and voice harmonize each other; front and behind accompany each other. Therefore the sage manages affairs without action and spreads doctrines without words.[12]

The Power (*De*)

For Laozi, *De* is the power and pattern of nature, the meaningful movement of the universe itself. *De*, which means power or virtue, describes the function or operation of *Dao*. It is the dynamic power of *Dao* inherent in individuals and nature. *De* is *Dao* in action.

Reversal and Return. *De* is the rhythm of nature, the endless ebb and flow of reversal and return. When a thing reaches one extreme, it reverts from it. If anything develops extreme tendencies, those inclinations inevitably return to become their opposites. This is the law of nature.

> Reversing is the movement of the *Dao*. Weakness is the function of *Dao*. All things in the world come from being. And being comes from nonbeing.[13] To go further and further means to revert again.[14] Diminish a thing and it will increase. Increase a thing and it will diminish.[15] Be hollow and one shall be filled. Be exhausted and one shall be renewed. Have little and one shall obtain.[16]

To the unenlightened mind, these sayings seem paradoxical, perplexing and puzzling—but to those who understand the law of nature, they make perfectly profound sense. The law of nature is the principle of change, but the principle itself is invariable, stable and eternal, without beginning or end. Laozi declared: "Not to know the invariable and to act blindly is to go to disaster."[17]

Enlightened Sages. Those who practice enlightenment, Laozi calls sages. Whether state ruler or rural farmer, anyone can become an enlightened-sage. Enlightenment involves knowing the laws of nature and performing daily activities accordingly.

> To know the invariable is called enlightenment. Whoever knows the invariable is free. Being free is without prejudice. Being without prejudice is comprehensive. Being comprehensive is vast. Being vast is being with the *Dao*. Being with the *Dao*, one survives and avoids harm.[18]

In practical terms, in order to attain something, one must enter through its opposite:

> In order to contract, it is necessary first to expand. In order to weaken, it is necessary first to strengthen. In order to destroy, it is necessary first to promote. In order to grasp, it is first necessary to give. The weak and the tender overcome the hard and the strong.[19]

Becoming strong begins with acknowledging weakness and recognizing that weakness overcomes strength. Strength fails where weakness prevails. Nature itself illustrates that strength is achieved through weakness. In a typhoon, tall trees are toppled while lowly bushes and blades of grass bend and blow in a hurricane unbroken. The wind has no form or body, but it can blow down buildings. Water, though soft and slippery, erodes mountains and culls canyons. "There is nothing softer or weaker than water, and yet there is nothing better for attacking hard and strong things."[20]

De, like *Dao*, is beyond words and conceptual understanding but it can be compared to water, which it resembles in three ways: it nurtures everything; it flows freely, and it seeks lowly places despised by people. "*De* is like water. Water benefits all creatures, while not contending with them. It resides in the places people find repugnant, and so, comes close to the *Dao*."[21] The sage, like the *Dao* itself, resembles water that seeks the lowest level. Sages humble themselves below others. As water nourishes all without contending, the sage serves everyone equally without prejudice or favoritism.

> The sage, staying in the background, is always out in front. Remaining outside, the sage is always there. The sage does not strive for any personal interest. Therefore, all his interests are fulfilled.[22] The sage does not make a display of himself, therefore is seen everywhere. The sage does not contend and therefore no one in the world can contend with the sage.[23]

The person who embodies *De* lives a simple, natural, peaceful life. A simple way of life means minimizing—not multiplying—desires. People are normally driven to fulfill their many desires. Conflicts arise because people must compete with each other for the limited resources to fulfill their ever-increasing whims and wishes. Rules of moral behavior are invented and introduced to regulate harmony and peace among people competing to fulfill their desires. Unfortunately, moral rules do not solve the problem; instead, they compound it because people break the rules resulting in increased contention and strife. Even though moral rules do not solve the problem, they cannot be abandoned unless desire, as the main motivation for action, is eliminated. The only way to abandon actions driven by desire is to adopt a simple way of life in harmony with nature.

Living naturally means being in tune with the universe and acting in harmony with the *Dao*. "There is no greater disaster than discontent; there is no greater crime than greed."[24] Laozi lived a simple, spontaneous life close to nature and far from preoccupations with wealth, fame or political power.

Which does one love more, fame or one's own life? Which is more valuable, one's own life or wealth? Which is worse, gain or loss? The one who has lavish desires will spend extravagantly. The one who hoards will lose heavily. The one who is contented suffers no disgrace. The one who knows when to stop is free from danger and lives long.[25]

In contrast to the Confucian prescription of deliberate ritual actions, Laozi practiced an inspired spontaneity called effortless-action (*wu-wei*). The Chinese character is a pictogram that combines two opposite symbols—extreme exertion and utmost relaxation. Its literal translation is non-action, which is misleading because *wu-wei* indicates a particular type of action that is not premeditated, artificial, assertive, aggressive, or forced. It is spontaneous action characterized by attentive, responsive adaptation to ever-changing circumstances.

Effortless-action describes the disposition of the doer. It refers to the ease of action inspired by tranquility. Laozi likens the sage's simplicity, spontaneity and tranquility to an infant. Babies act automatically without thought or intention.

Simplicity, which has no name, is free of desires. Being free of desires, it is tranquil.[26] Therefore let people hold on to these: embrace simplicity, reduce selfishness and have few desires.[27]

Summary

Laozi was a non-conformist who felt estranged and alienated from a society into which he did not fit or feel at home. The 20th chapter of the *Daodejing* may be an autobiographic expression of Laozi's sense of himself in relation to a civilization crumbling all around him:

I alone am inert, showing no sign of desires, like an infant that has not yet smiled. Wearied, indeed, I seem to be without a home. The multitude all possess more than enough. I alone seem to have lost all. Mine is indeed the mind of an ignorant man, indiscriminate and dull! Common folks are indeed brilliant; I alone seem to be in the dark. Common folks see differences and are clear-cut. I alone make no distinctions. I seem drifting as at sea; like the wind blowing about, seemingly without destination. The multitude all have a purpose; I alone seem to be stubborn and rustic. I alone differ from others, and value drawing sustenance from Mother *Dao*.[28]

Laozi laments but does not despair the paradoxical predicament in which he finds himself:

My doctrines are very easy to understand and very easy to practice, but none in the world can understand or practice them. The source of my doctrines is nature and the master of my deed is *Dao*. It is because people do not understand this that they do not understand me. Few people know me and therefore I am highly valued.[29]

Between Laozi and Jesus

Jesus exhibited several traits of Laozi's sage, the unassuming servant, who sacrifices himself for the sake of others, and Laozi embodied characteristics of Jesus, especially his humility. Laozi and Jesus were both anti-establishment; they were renouncers of the world orders in which they lived. Laozi longed for a return to the pre-civilized, natural order while Jesus announced and inaugurated the kingdom of God on earth. Both men spoke in enigmatic sayings and perplexing profundities. The meanings of Laozi's poems are hidden in paradox just as some of the teachings of Jesus are veiled in parables. They were each keen observers of nature and drew life lessons from it, but while Jesus displayed power over nature, Laozi harmonized and identified with its infinite plentitude.

The *Dao* of Laozi is not the same as the way, truth and life that Jesus claimed to be. Laozi's *Dao* is the way of nature, its cyclical source and sole sustainer. While Laozi declares the *Dao* to be unutterable and without origin, the *Gospel of John* declares Jesus to be the divine word that became flesh. Jesus is not the Son of Mother Nature, but the Son of God who has authority over nature to command the wind, calm the waves, walk on water or change it into wine.

Between *Dao* and God

The *Dao* of Laozi is not the God and father of Jesus. *Dao* may transcend words but it does not transcend the nature of the universe itself. The God and father of Jesus is not reducible to the forces and factors of nature. While imminent and operative in nature and history, God is also exalted above the heavens and utterly transcends everything whatsoever that is not God. On the contrary, the *Dao* is always only imminent, all-encompassing, all-embracing, excluding nothing. The sage who embodies *Dao* lives above distinguishing between good and evil. "If all people of the world know that beauty is beauty, there is already ugliness. If all people of the world know that good is good, there is already evil."[30]

For Jesus good and evil are not relative values to be transcended, abandoned or determined on the basis of balance between natural polar forces.
Opposing cosmic forces between good and evil are irreconcilable; they are
neither complementary nor cooperative. The essence of one is not present in
the center of the other; when one becomes excessive, it does not reverse to its
opposite. They are absolutely incompatible. God is light in whom there is no
darkness at all.[31] Jesus came to demarcate the difference between the realm of
light and darkness, the domain of Satan and the kingdom of God. Jesus came
casting out demons and dispelling disease as a sign that the kingdom had
come. There can be no compromise or communion between forces of good
and evil.

What Christians Might Learn From Laozi

Contentment in Simplicity

Christians might learn from Laozi to minimize and moderate desires. Laozi,
like Jesus, called people to a life of simplicity and contentment. The abundant
life that Jesus promised is not a wishing well of desires fulfilled.[32] Jesus prescribed a simple way of life for his disciples and constantly cautioned the rich
about the dangers and snares of wealth. Jesus identified and associated mostly
with the poor and marginalized members of society. It is easy to overlook the
fact that Jesus was a man of very few desires who lived the simplest of all life-
styles. Not a homeowner, he often slept under the stars, shared bread, and ate
fish caught by his companions.

The abundant life is not to be confused with lavish living. Jesus said:
"Blessed are the poor, for theirs is the kingdom of God." Citizens of Christ's
kingdom are characterized by contentment that does not come through the
fulfillment of many desires but by faith in God who knows about their needs,
even before they ask.[33] Thus the Christian's contentment comes from the
comfort and consolation of communion with Christ—not from the fulfillment
of wishes or the acquisition of many possessions.

Befriending Nature

Christians can learn from Laozi to think of nature as a friend with whom to
live in harmony rather than a force or foe to combat and conquer. From Laozi,
Christians can learn the paramount importance of living simply in harmony

LAOZI 85

with the environment rather than exploiting, polluting and destroying it. Befriending nature might mean harmoniously harnessing her sustainable and renewable sources of energy like sun, wind and water rather than rupturing and ravaging the earth by drilling and fracking for fossil fuels. It might mean recycling products for reproduction rather than discarding and depositing poisons and pollutants into soil, water and air.

In the Garden of Eden, God commissioned humanity to cultivate and care for the earth.[34] As vice-regents with Jesus, Christians have dominion over the whole creation—however dominion does not mean domination, depletion or deforestation. Sharing custody over God's creation is a call for Christians to exercise ecological concern for the environment. Christian ecology is the stewardship of the habitat where humanity and all creation live and move and enjoy their being. Christians are primarily custodians—not consumers—and the earth is not a commodity to be consumed but a garden and sanctuary in which to discover and adore God. The earth is the Lord's footstool and humanity's sacred space for service and worship.

Words to the Wise

Laozi offers three parting pieces of advice that make particularly good sense for Christians. First, "Pleasant words are not true. True words are not pleasant."[35] The gospel presents an inconvenient truth; it paints an unpopular and unpleasant picture of the human predicament. It declares that people are sinful and separated from God. The gospel is good news only because it overcomes the bad news that death is the consequence of sin; the good news is that eternal life is the free gift of God through Jesus Christ.

Second, "The good person does not argue. The person who argues is not good."[36] Christian testimony can be confrontational without being contentious. Christians are called to be ready to defend their faith whenever anyone asks them to give an account. The great commission involves taking the initiative to present the gospel to the world. Christians can communicate their faith without being combative. People must be compelled, convinced and converted to enter the kingdom of God, but no one gains entry by losing an argument to a Christian.

Laozi's famous last words are also well worth remembering. "Those who know are not learned. Those who are learned do not know."[37] Ironically, Laozi himself was a learned man. As the emperor's librarian, he read many books. The knowledge Laozi writes about is not book learning and not obtainable by formal education. Laozi whispers about a wisdom that comes from his direct, personal experience, not from intellectual or academic achievement.

Jesus had no formal education. We know he could read because he read from the scroll in the synagogue. Apart from a spurious scripture that says he once scratched a sign in the dirt, there is no evidence that he could write.[38] He was the son of a carpenter. The gospel is simple and easy to comprehend; it does not appeal to the sophisticated mind. "Unless you change and become like little children, you will not enter the kingdom of God."[39] There is no intelligence quotient necessary to grasp the gospel or respond to its call; the only knowledge necessary for entrance into the kingdom of God is knowledge of God revealed in Jesus:

> I praise you, Lord, father of heaven and earth, because you have hidden these things from the wise and learned and revealed them unto little children. Yes, Father, for that is what you were pleased to do. All things have been committed to me by my Father. No one knows the Son except the Father and no one knows the Father except the Son and those to whom the Son chooses to reveal him.[40]

Notes

1. *Daodejing* 42, "The Natural Way of Lao-tzu," in *A Source Book in Chinese Philosophy* compiled and translated by Wing-Tsit Chan, Princeton University Press, 1963. All references to the *Daodejing* are based on this translation unless otherwise noted.
2. Qian, Sima, *Shiji: Records of the Grand Historian,* translated by Burton Watson, Columbia University Press, 1996.
3. Qian, Sima, *Shiji: Records of the Grand Historian.*
4. Graham, A. C., *Disputers of the Tao: Philosophical Argument in Ancient China,* Open Court Publishers, 1989.
5. *Daodejing* 1.
6. *Daodejing* 56.
7. *Daodejing* 41.
8. *Daodejing* 1.
9. *Daodejing* 25.
10. *Daodejing* 10; 56; 81.
11. *Daodejing* 11.
12. *Daodejing* 2.
13. *Daodejing* 40.
14. *Daodejing* 45.
15. *Daodejing* 42.
16. *Daodejing* 22.
17. *Daodejing* 16.

18. *Daodejing* 16.
19. *Daodejing* 36.
20. *Daodejing* 78.
21. *Daodejing* 8.
22. *Daodejing* 7.
23. *Daodejing* 22.
24. *Daodejing* 46.
25. *Daodejing* 44.
26. *Daodejing* 37.
27. *Daodejing* 19.
28. *Daodejing* 20.
29. *Daodejing* 70.
30. *Daodejing* 2.
31. *I John* 1:5, *Holy Bible: New International Version*, Zondervan Publishers, 1984. All references to the Bible are based on this translation unless otherwise noted.
32. *John* 10:10.
33. *Luke* 12:27.
34. *Genesis* 2:15.
35. *Daodejing* 81.
36. *Daodejing* 81.
37. *Daodejing* 81.
38. *John* 8:8.
39. *Matthew* 18:3.
40. *Matthew* 11:25–27.

· 6 ·

MOSES

Introduction

Moses liberated the Jews from slavery in Egypt and established Israel as an independent theocratic federation of tribes. Moreover, he established Judaism as a universal religion, inviting all humanity to worship a single sovereign God. As recipient and mediator of the 10 commandments, Moses is the ancient architect of ethics and inadvertent father of many modern civilizations governed by the rule of law.

Although Judaism has historically developed into distinctly different traditional ways of interpretation and practice, all respect Moses as the man responsible for mediating and instituting the copious and comprehensive rules and regulations that define and guide Judaism. Of the numerous ancient Near-Eastern national religions, only Judaism endures into the present day.

Its survival is especially astounding in view of the fact that Jews have been the victims of mass executions and genocidal campaigns repeatedly throughout their harrowing history. In 1948, after the execution of 6,000,000 Jews by Hitler's Germany, global conscience moved the United Nations to re-establish and return the ancient promised land to a restored and independently political Israel. Today Jews continue to suffer the atrocities of persecution due to aggressive hostility and hatred perpetuated throughout the world. Despite innumerable adversities, Jews have made monumental contributions to the intellectual and cultural history of the world. Karl Marx, Sigmund Freud and Albert Einstein are just a few of the Jewish intellectual giants whose ideas have profoundly influenced the world.

Socio-political Context

Egyptian society during the life of Moses was hierarchically structured in the form of a pyramid. At the pinnacle of political power and social privilege, the pharaoh was regarded as a human embodiment of divinity and ruled the nation with absolute authority. His or her will was law. Immediately beneath the pharaoh were viziers, government officials, priests, scribes and nobles; below them were soldiers who acted as administrators of public works in times of peace; lower still were the artisans and merchants; at the bottom level were peasant farmers and slaves who comprised the vast majority of the population that labored in poverty to support the privileged minority.

The social hierarchy was divinely sanctioned and ordered by the principle of Ma'at, which means harmony, and balance. Ma'at was the universal principle which allowed the world to function harmoniously and the social hierarchy of ancient Egypt was believed to reflect it. The primary responsibility of the pharaoh was to maintain Ma'at. Religion in ancient Egypt was a complex cosmological monotheism which accepted other gods as powers responsible for specific realms of operation under the supervision of the one and only transcendent god. It was a monotheism that maintained belief in the one god in relation to the many.[1] Moses introduced his God in complete contradistinction to all the powers and principalities of Egypt. Moses forged Judaism in stark contrast to the Egyptian culture that constituted the socio-political context of its birth. In sharp contrast to the religion of the pharaohs, the monotheism of Moses establishes the equality and dignity of all human beings created in the image of God, regardless of class, race, gender, ethnicity or national identity.

Texts as Context

Jewish tradition attributes authorship of the first five books of the Bible, known in Hebrew as the *Torah*, to Moses. While acknowledging Moses as responsible for its core, many text-historical critics contend it was composed by several sources until it was compiled into its final form in the fifth century BCE.

The book of *Genesis* provides the backstory for the Jew's exodus from Egypt and the literary context for the life and teachings of Moses. It is arranged in four literary blocks beginning with the creation of the world to the call of Abraham. The second section narrates the sojourn of Abraham from his establishment of a covenant with God to his death. The third and fourth sections feature the patriarchal narratives of Abraham's descendants, particularly of Isaac and Jacob but also of his son Joseph, who established residence in Egypt under protection of the pharaoh. Judaism identifies its heritage through Abraham's grandson Jacob, whose name was changed to Israel to commemorate his struggle with the angel of God.[2] Israel means "one who strives with God." Jacob had 12 sons with two wives and two maidservants whose descendants make up the dozen tribes that comprise the nation. Israel is both the name of Jacob and the nation that descends from him.

The book of *Exodus* begins with an explanation of how Abraham's descendants lapsed into Egyptian slavery when the newly enthroned pharaoh, fearing the growing size and threat of the immigrant Hebrew population, pressed them into service for public building projects. *Exodus* narrates the liberation from Egyptian slavery, Moses' reception and mediation of the 10 commandments at Mount Sinai, and the beginning of Israel's 40-year period of wandering through the wilderness en route to the land that God had promised in covenant to Abraham and his descendants.

The book of *Leviticus* focuses on the role of the Levites, the tribe descended from Levi, one of the 12 sons of Israel. Designated as priests, they were charged with teaching the people the difference between ritual purity and pollution. *Leviticus* spells out the holiness code of conduct by which Israel is to distinguish itself as God's holy people.[3]

The book of *Numbers* is so named because it begins with a military census of the tribes of Israel. Spies are sent into Canaan to assess the prospects for a successful invasion, but because they return with a discouraging report, the Israelites must wander in the wilderness and postpone their entrance into the promised land for an additional 38 years. The Hebrew name of the book is *Bemidbar*, which means wanderings, because it chronicles God's intervention, protection and guidance despite the people's infidelity, insubordination and incessant complaining about the harsh conditions during the wilderness wanderings.

The book of *Deuteronomy*, literally a copy of the law, is Moses' interpretation of Israel's identity and destiny from Mount Sinai to beyond the Jordan River to the brink of the promised land of Canaan. The book contains the reception of the many communal laws, and spells out the ethical, economic, ritual and social way of life Israel must lead to preserve its political existence. It concludes with Moses' ritual renewal of the covenant between God and Israel, appointing Joshua as successor, blessing the tribes of Israel, and a narrative on the death and burial of Moses. By the end of *Deuteronomy*, Israel is poised to enter the promised land.

Backstory, Birth, and Youth

Moses was born in Egypt to Hebrew slaves, Jochabed and Amram, about 1,400 years before Christ. He entered history during a systematic program of genocide aimed at all newborn Hebrew boys. The pharaoh felt threatened by the rapidly growing population of immigrant Hebrew slaves whom he feared would revolt.[4] In a scheme to save Moses from the pharaoh's program of genocide, Moses' mother, Amram, hid the child for the first three months until he was too big to conceal. Then, his mother placed the infant in a crude basket which she interred and entrusted in the marshy reeds of the Nile River. Following along the banks, Moses' sister, Miriam, tracked the floating basket downstream. By providential fortune, the pharaoh's daughter was performing her morning bathing rituals on the bank and discovered the baby drifting by. She ordered her attendant to fetch the basket from the river. The moment she saw the child, she adored and adopted him as her own son. She named him Moses, which means "drawn from the river."[5]

Meanwhile Moses' sister Miriam, witnessing the water rescue, approached the princess and offered to find a Hebrew woman to serve as a wet nurse for her new-found son. Moses' sister cleverly recruited the baby's mother, Amram, to nurse and nurture her own son until he was old enough to wean and return to the princess. After several years of childhood instruction in the Hebrew traditions under his parent's custody, Moses was raised in the Egyptian palace, where he received a privileged, princely education in the arts and sciences of Egypt.

Exile, Revelation, and Return

Heir to a mixed heritage of Hebrew and Egyptian cultures, Moses primarily identified and empathized with his fellow Hebrews who were enslaved by the very same power that gave him princely privilege. He was raised in a confluence of continual conflicts of personal identity. One day the struggle to balance the split of cultural identities proved too much for Moses. When he saw an Egyptian slave-master mistreating a fellow Hebrew, he snapped. Thinking that no one was watching, Moses struck and unintentionally killed the Egyptian slave-master. Unfortunately there were witnesses, and when confronted with his crime, Moses fled from Egypt in fear for his life and took refuge on the back side of the Midian desert. There he met and married Zipporah, with whom he fathered sons and daughters. For the next 50 years, Moses served his father-in-law by herding his sheep and tending his goats.

One day Moses was grazing the flocks when a bush, ablaze with the fiery figure of the Lord's angel, arrested his attention. Moses was spellbound by the surreal sight. From out of the flaming bush, Moses heard the voice of God addressing him:

> Moses, Moses! He responded: Here I am. The Lord continued: Don't come any further. Take the shoes off your feet because the ground on which you stand is holy. Then the Lord said, I am the God of your father, the God of Abraham, Isaac and Jacob.[6]

God's self-identification recalls the covenant promise to Abraham. The Hebrew word for covenant (berit) comes from a verbal root meaning to cut, which refers to the ancient custom of sealing treaties with a dismemberment ceremony. When the covenant with Abraham was ratified, he was directed to bring several birds and animals, cut them in half and place the halves opposite each other to form an aisle.[7] Normally, ancient Near-Eastern treaties between kings required the subordinate party to parade between the cut carcasses to symbolize their acceptance of the same fate if they failed to live up to the terms of the covenant; however, instead of requiring Abraham to march between the pieces, a potted pillar of smoke and fire appeared and passed through the aisle of corpses, signifying God's self-submission to the same fate were God unfaithful in fulfilling the covenant promises. Just as God appeared and passed before Abraham in the form of fire and smoke, so God arrested and addressed Moses from within the fiery bush.

Moses bowed his head low into the dust of the desert because he was afraid to look at the glory of God. Moses was told that God had heard the cries of the enslaved descendants of Abraham and was deeply concerned about them. God commissioned Moses to return to Egypt to negotiate with the pharaoh for the liberation of the Hebrew slaves. Moses responded with reluctance, protesting that he was not the right man for such a momentous mission. Moses disqualified and exempted himself with an effacing self-assessment. "But who am I that I should go to pharaoh and lead the Israelites out of Egypt?" Moses further reacted with a litany of what-ifs. "What if they don't believe me? What if they ask who sent me, who shall I say you are?"[8]

The Lord said to Moses: "I am who I am; tell them 'I am' sent you."[9] In Hebrew the verb "I am" sounds strikingly similar to the Hebrew word for Lord. God equipped Moses with miraculous signs to perform as proof for the people to believe, and since Moses insisted that he was an inept speaker, God consented to allow his brother Aaron to serve as Moses' mouthpiece.[10]

Exodus From Egypt

When Moses returned to Egypt, his brother Aaron went out to meet him. Moses told Aaron everything that had happened and all the Lord had said. Moses and Aaron then assembled all the Hebrews together and Aaron explained all about God's revealed strategy to rescue them from slavery and to lead them to the land as promised in the covenant with Abraham.[11]

By a series of miraculous signs and wonders, including 10 intense and timely natural disasters, Moses, with Aaron's assistance, persuaded the pharaoh to let the Hebrews leave Egypt.[12] The plague that finally broke the pharaoh's stubborn will was the death of all the first-born males of Egypt. God identified the newly-forming nation of Israel as God's first-born son. Because the pharaoh threatened to kill God's first-born son, therefore God threatened the lives of all first-born males in Egypt. In order to avoid the death of all Israelite first-born males, Moses instructed them to do as God directed: each household was to sacrifice a lamb and smear a smattering of its blood on the doorposts of their homes. When the angel of death came to slay the first-born males of Egypt, the angel passed over the blood-marked dwellings of the Hebrews and let them live.[13]

After their successful escape, the pharaoh had a change of heart and set himself against God and the Hebrews. The pharaoh's horses, chariots and army pursued the Hebrew slaves, hoping to capture and corral them back to Egypt. Moses, employing a strategy calculated to confound the pharaoh, stationed his people on the edge of the Red Sea. As the Egyptian army approached, God took up a position between the two forces in the form of a billowing pillar of cloud. To the Egyptians the cloud appeared dark and foreboding, shielding the Hebrews from sight—but the Hebrews saw bright flashing peels of light from the cloud which continually illuminated the night sky. During the night while the armies camped, strong winds divided the waves of the sea into two walls, thereby creating a dry riverbed leading across the sea to the other side. Moses led his people through the dry pathway onto the banks beyond; however, when the Egyptian horses, chariots and soldiers followed in pursuit, they were drowned in the deluge of the mighty waters rushing back into the riverbed.[14]

Once safely on the other shore, Moses led the people to the mountain to worship God. Moses ascended the mountain to meet with God in the cloud that hovered and covered its peak. From within the cloud, God forged a covenant with Moses and his new-found federation of tribes.[15]

Idolatry

After mediating the 10 commandments (see Teachings) to the people, Moses received further revelations directing him to prepare the people for a formal ritual oath ceremony to ratify the treaty imposed by God. Having instructed the people to wait at the foot of the mountain for his return, Moses ascended again to meet with God in the foreboding cloud covering the top of the mountain. During Moses' absence the people quickly grew impatient and imagined that Moses had disappeared or abandoned them. They clamored to Aaron for the guidance and guardianship of some reliable god that could lead them out of their wilderness wanderings. Seeking to oblige them, Aaron ordered them to bring him their precious gold jewelry, which he melted and molded into the shape of a calf. Then they began worshipping the young bull and celebrating in riotous revelry.

When Moses descended the mountain, he witnessed the idolatrous display of debauchery, decadence and disloyalty to the Lord who had just delivered them from the hands of their oppressors. Inflamed with righteous rage, Moses smashed the tablets on the ground, pulverized the golden calf, spread the powder into the water, and forced the people to drink it.[16]

Also erupting in righteous indignation, God was poised to punish the people with the permanency of annihilation—but Moses intervened, persuading God to relent and receive the people back into protective custody and care. Moved by the mediation of Moses, and for the sake of the promise sworn to Abraham and his descendants, God granted grace and forgiveness to Moses and his motley mob.[17]

Tablets, Ark, and Tent-Temple

A short time later, Moses again climbed the mountain to meet with God in the shroud of the cloud. Moses was reissued the covenant on tablets engraved by God's own finger.[18] The details revealed to Moses on the mountain included architectural plans for a portable ark in which to keep the covenant tablets, and a portable tent-temple made of an elaborate array of ornate curtains, poles, posts and pegs in which to house the ark and meet with God. Moses also received a comprehensive slate of rules and regulations to guide and govern Jewish social and spiritual culture. The legal corpus included instructions on the observance of annual holidays and festivals, especially Passover which commemorates the deliverance from Egypt. Moses returned from the mountain with the two tablets, then ritually recited and ratified the covenant with an oath ceremony culminating in sacrifices and the sprinkling of blood on the heads of the assembled people as a solemn sign of their submission to its terms.[19]

In this way, God initiated an alliance with the nation of Israel just as other ancient nations entered into covenantal relationships with each other. Moses represented God as the supreme sovereign potentate of the universe and himself as the mediator of God's wide-ranging political and spiritual power. While all the other nations had a human king to lead and guide them, Moses taught that God alone was both king and shepherd to Israel.

Whenever Moses entered the portable tent-temple, the people could see him disappear into the enveloping cloud of God's glory. The *Torah* says Moses spoke with God just as friends meet together face to face.[20] Whenever Moses came out of the tent and returned to the camp, his face shone so radiantly from having been in the presence of God that he had to wear a veil to cover his face from public view. The brightness of Moses' face is but a faint reflection of the blinding glare of God's glorious face. Whenever Moses and Aaron met with God, they covered their eyes and hid their faces because they believed no one could see God's face and live to tell about it.[21]

Wandering in the Wilderness

For the next 40 years Moses herded the newly-fashioned federation while they wandered around in the wilderness following the Lord's lead from within a cloud by day and a pillar of fire by night. The people groaned and complained incessantly about the hardships of desert life, but Moses faithfully sought out God to miraculously provide for their most basic needs. To quench their thirst, he extracted water from a rock by striking it with his rod on God's command. To satisfy their hunger, God provided bread from above as well as flocks of quail in quantities sufficient for each day's need.[22]

When the people again complained of thirst, God directed Moses to take his rod and assemble the people in front of a rock. God instructed Moses to publicly command the rock to gush forth water. Instead of speaking to the rock, Moses seethed and spewed sarcastic words of criticism at the people and smacked the rock with his rod to send forth a steady stream of water for them to drink.[23] By failing to acknowledge God's hand in the miracle, Moses created the dramatic impression that he himself brought forth water from the rock. For refusing to follow God's simple instruction, Moses was prohibited from entering the promised land when God said to him, "This is the land I promised on oath to Abraham, Isaac and Jacob when I said, 'I will give it to your descendants.' I have let you see it with your eyes, but you will not cross over into it."[24]

Death and Legacy

On the last day of his life, Moses blessed each tribe of Israel, recited the entire law to the assembled nation, and appointed Joshua as his successor. He warned Joshua that the people would be rebellious, and spoke these final words:

> Take to heart all the words I have solemnly declared to you this day, so that you may command your children to obey carefully all the words of this law. They are not just idle words for you—they are your life.[25]

Moses died before the first campaign to conquer the promised land began. This land, flowing with milk and honey, was already occupied by Canaanites, Hittites, Jebusites, and several other ethnicities. Before he died, Moses gave his mantle and rod to Joshua, under whose guidance Israel claimed its inheritance by invading and gradually infiltrating, populating and cultivating the land promised long ago to Abraham and his descendants.

And Moses the servant of God died there in Moab, as the LORD had said. He buried him in Moab, in the valley opposite Beth Peor, but to this day no one knows where his grave is. Moses was 120 when he died, yet his eyes were not weak, nor his strength gone.[26]

Teachings

God's Covenant With Israel

According to one rabbinic tradition, 70 other nations had already rejected God's offer of the covenant before Israel finally accepted it under the threat of being crushed to death by the very mountain from which Moses received it.[27] Another tradition teaches that the reception of the 10 commandments was so crucial that the world would have come to an end had Israel not accepted them. Moses does not boast of any redeeming qualities in himself or Israel; instead he acknowledges God's merciful initiative, intervention and deliverance. Moreover, the entire biography of Moses dramatizes the mercy and power of God, not the strength or virtue of Moses, who stutters, babbles and blunders at every turn of events. He is a foil and instrument through whom God's glorious might and mercy are displayed. Nevertheless, Moses is a founder of faith in God's unity, justice, mercy and loving kindness.

The 10 commandments were cast in the same form as other ancient Near-Eastern treaties between nations. Kings forged covenants with each other for mutual protection and support. Some treaties were entered into freely between kings of equal power but others were imposed by powerful suzerain kings on their conquered and subjugated vassal nations. God's covenant with Israel followed the latter format, featuring God as the great suzerain king who imposes the terms and conditions, spelling out blessings for loyal obedience and curses for idolatrous betrayal.

Ancient Near-Eastern treaties followed a uniform formula, beginning with a preamble, followed by a historical prologue, then stipulations, commands, and conditions of reward and punishment.[28] The 10 commandments conform to this pattern. The preamble begins with a declaration of the suzerain king's greatness in terms of the size of his domain, and the number of chariots, horses, soldiers and artillery under his command. It is designed to instill a sense of awe, terror and dread in the hearts of its recipients and to remind them that the great king possesses military power sufficient to eradicate them from the face of the earth. The preamble of God's covenant with Israel is short and pointed, accomplishing the same purpose: "I am the Lord, your God."[29]

The historical prologue is a retelling of the acts of protection and support provided in the past by the suzerain king to his vassal treaty recipients. It reminds the recipients of all the beneficial and benevolent things the suzerain king has done for them in the past. It is calculated to make the recipients of the treaty grateful, which properly prepares them to receive the forthcoming commands and conditions. The historical prologue to the 10 commandments completes the document's opening statement: "who brought you up out of the land of Egypt, out of the house of bondage."[30]

Having properly prepared the recipients with a due sense of fear and gratitude, the next section sets the terms of the treaty. The first stipulation typically called for exclusive, undivided allegiance that precluded making any other treaties with any other kings. Similarly, God prohibits Israel from making alliances with any other gods.[31]

By Jewish reckoning, the first commandment enjoins faith in God's eternal existence and unbounded power. Although the first commandment is issued in the form of a statement rather than an imperative, rabbinic tradition explains that acknowledgment of God's sovereignty is prerequisite to accepting subsequent commands. Since God is invisible and has no form, God self-identifies as the one who has been revealed to Israel by miraculously delivering them from Egyptian slavery. God is made known in and through historical events. The people of Israel had witnessed and experienced the power of God firsthand.

The second commandment prohibits idolatry and comprises four distinct negative injunctions. It is forbidden to believe in idols, manufacture, possess or worship them. Adherence to this commandment radically distinguished Israel from Egypt and all the nations that surrounded them.

The third commandment prohibits vain oaths. Invoking God's name to advance one's own personal profit or private interest violates the spirit of this law. Equating one's own word with the veracity of God is conceited and contemptuous.

The fourth commandment mandates memory and observance of the sabbath. It requires remembering that God is the creator by respecting the seventh day. It serves as a regular reminder that God created for six days and rested on the seventh.

The fifth commandment obliges children to honor their parents. Rabbinic tradition observes that it takes three to produce a child: mother, father and God. Whereas the first four commandments directed honor to God, this one also honors God by reverencing parents. Honor entails actions that bring comfort and dignity to parents. Respect for parents is a cornerstone of faith in the *Torah* because it assures the perpetual observance of all the commandments since they are passed on from parents to children inter-generationally.

The sixth commandment prohibits murder. The rabbis interpreted killing broadly and taught that the commandment extends far beyond the illegal taking of life, including causing someone significant embarrassment, neglecting to provide food and safety for travelers, and causing someone to lose their livelihood.

The seventh commandment forbids adultery. The person who is unfaithful to a spouse betrays God's trust. Adultery, like idolatry, ruptures the relationship.

The eighth commandment is a prohibition against stealing. According to rabbinical tradition, it refers specifically to a kidnapper who forces his victim to work for him and then sells him into slavery. This conclusion is reached through a method of interpretation that treats the passage according to its context. Since one who violates the previous prohibitions in this same verse—murder and adultery—is liable to the death penalty, this commandment must also involve such an offense. The kidnapper case described above is the only theft that warrants death. Nevertheless, other rabbis extended the commandment to include forms of behavior related to theft. For example, failure to respond to a greeting is theft of a person's self-esteem and to win someone's gratitude or respect through deceit is a form of thievery.

The ninth commandment prohibits bearing false witness. It refers to providing false or misleading testimony in a court of law but rabbinical interpretation extends it to include gossip and slander.

The tenth commandment is against coveting. Rabbinic tradition notes that this final commandment is one that only a divine lawgiver could have decreed. A human ruler can only enact and enforce laws that apply to external behavior, whereas God's claim extends even to a person's thoughts and attitudes.[32]

Between Moses and Jesus

Moses is so crucial to the significance of Jesus that it is no exaggeration to say that Jesus' mission and message cannot be fully appreciated without understanding the life and teachings of Moses. Jesus said: If you believed Moses, you would believe me because he wrote about me.[33] Jesus was referring to the words Moses spoke to the Israelites in the wilderness: "The Lord your God will raise up a prophet like me from among you, from your fellow Israelites. You must listen to him."[34]

The *Gospel of Matthew* presents Jesus as the new Moses who leads an exodus to deliver people from slavery to sin. Just as Moses' parents protected him from the pharaoh's infanticide, Jesus' parents fled with him to Egypt to escape King Herod's decree to kill all newborn Hebrew boys. Matthew cites these parallels between Moses and Jesus when he recalls the ancient Hebrew prophecy where God says: "Out of Egypt, I will call my Son."[35]

Just as Moses climbed Mount Sinai and sat down to receive the 10 commandments, Jesus ascended the mountain and sat down to deliver his interpretation of the Mosaic law.[36] Jesus' interpretation exposes and addresses the invisible intentions and hidden motives of the heart. It is not that Jesus holds people to a higher standard than Moses did; Jesus neither raises nor lowers the bar. He does not intend to make it more difficult to enter the kingdom of God; rather, his interpretation aims to expose the impossibility of entering the kingdom by fulfilling God's law, not because of any deficiency in the law but because people are sinful.

Regarding the law of Moses and the pronouncements of prophets, Jesus said: "Do not think that I have come to abolish the Law or the Prophets; I have not come to abolish them but to fulfill them."[37] To his Jewish adversaries Jesus said: "You search the Scriptures because in them you think you have eternal life; and it is they that bear witness about me, yet you refuse to come to me that you may have life."[38]

Jesus identified himself with the memorial name that God revealed to Moses at the burning bush. In a confrontational encounter with his opponents, Jesus said:

> Whoever obeys my word will never see death. His opponents protested: Are you greater than our father Abraham? He died and so did the prophets. Who do you think you are? Jesus answered: Your father Abraham rejoiced at the thought of seeing my day; he saw it and was glad. His opponents replied: You are not yet fifty years old, and you have seen Abraham? Jesus answered: Before Abraham was born, I am.[39]

The daily bread found fresh in the wilderness on the ground each morning under Moses' leadership was believed by some rabbis to be an edible and nourishing form of God. Jesus reminded the Jews how they received bread from heaven in the wilderness and then publicly proclaimed himself to be the bread of life that descends from heaven. "For the bread of God is he who comes down from heaven and gives life to the world."[40]

The night that Jesus was betrayed, he observed Passover in Jerusalem with his disciples. During that ceremony, Jesus identified the unleavened bread with his own body, broken for the forgiveness of sin; he also identified the wine as a sign of the new covenant sealed with his own blood.[41] Just as the blood of sacrificial lambs smeared on the doorposts in Egypt delivered Israelites from the angel of death, the blood Jesus shed when crucified rescues people from bondage to sin.

Jesus compares his sacrificial death on the cross to the bronze serpent that Moses raised on a pole in the wilderness to heal those bitten by poisonous snakes. "So Moses made a bronze snake and put it on a pole. Then when anyone was bitten by a snake, and looked at the bronze snake, they lived."[42] Jesus said: "Just as Moses lifted up the snake so the son of Man must be lifted up that everyone who believes may have eternal life in him."[43]

What Christians Might Learn From Moses

From Moses, Christians can learn how to lead a successful civil rights movement. The Reverend Dr. Martin Luther King Jr. drew inspiration from the movement Moses led. Dr. King's "I have a dream" speech reaches its crescendo in his rhetorical use of the mountain top from which Moses looked and saw the promised land. Dr. King's dream of racial harmony went beyond economic and social equality to envision the empathetic embrace of all races by each other. Moses can serve as an inspiring example and motivating model for civil rights activists and advocates to effect significant social, economic and political change for the benefit of all kinds of disadvantaged and disenfranchised members of society.

From Moses, Christians can learn that the power and authority for effective spiritual leadership is grounded in humble service. Moses' civil rights strategy was rooted in God's law and human responsibilities. The Israelites were liberated, not merely for the sake of freedom, but in order to serve humanity in obedience to God. Christians who aspire to positions of leadership, whether pastoral or political, would be wise to make Moses their model since he had the character qualities essential for successful leadership. At first glance, many might conclude that Moses did not possess the qualities to be a good leader since he was unassertive, lacked self-confidence, had no public speaking skills, and was reticent to act. Yet Moses was a good leader because he was a good follower; the secret is that they are the same thing. To lead people, especially in ways of peace, love and truth, one must follow God. Moses followed God around in circles, wandering in the wilderness for 40 years, but was nevertheless able to point the people to a place beyond where he himself was able to go.

Notes

1. Assmann, J., *Monotheismus und Kosmotheismus: Agyptische Formen eines "Denkens des Einen" und ihre europaische Rezeptionsgeschichte*, Heidelberg: Winter, 1993.
2. *Genesis* 32:22–32, *Holy Bible: New International Version*, Zondervan Publishers, 1984. All Bible references are from this translation unless otherwise noted.
3. *Leviticus* 1:10; 15:31.
4. *Exodus* 1:8.
5. *Exodus* 2:2–10.
6. *Exodus* 3:5.
7. *Genesis* 15:9–21.
8. *Exodus* 3:13.
9. *Exodus* 3:14.
10. *Exodus* 4:14–16.
11. *Exodus* 4:27–30.
12. *Exodus* 7:14–11:10.
13. *Exodus* 12:23.
14. *Exodus* 14.
15. *Exodus* 19.
16. *Exodus* 32.
17. *Exodus* 32:11–14.
18. *Exodus* 34:1–4.
19. *Exodus* 34–37.
20. *Exodus* 33:11.
21. *Exodus* 33:20.
22. *Exodus* 16.
23. *Numbers* 20:11.
24. *Deuteronomy* 32:52.
25. *Deuteronomy* 32:46.
26. *Deuteronomy* 34:4–7.
27. *Babylonian Talmud: Tractate Sanhedrin*, R. Avdimi b., Chama b. Chasa, b. Shab. 88a (Exegesis of *Exodus* 19:17), translated into English by Jacob Shachter and H. Freedman, Edited by I. Epstein, 1987.
28. Kline, Meredith G., *Treaty of the Great King: The Covenant Structure of Deuteronomy*, William B. Eerdmans, 1963.

29. *Exodus* 20:2.

30. *Exodus* 20:2.

31. *Exodus* 20:3–5.

32. Scherman, Rabbi Nosson, *The Chumash: The Torah: Haftaros and Five Megillos with a Commentary Anthologized from the Rabbinic Writings,* Mesorah Publications, Ltd., New York, 2015.

33. John 5:46, *Holy Bible: New International Version,* Zondervan Publishers, 1984. All Bible references are from this translation unless otherwise noted.

34. *Deuteronomy* 18:15.

35. *Matthew* 2:15; *Hosea* 11:1.

36. *Matthew* 5–7.

37. *Matthew* 5:17–18.

38. *John* 5:39–40.

39. *John* 8:48–59.

40. *John* 6:36.

41. *Matthew* 26:26–27.

42. *Numbers* 21:9.

43. *John* 3:14–15.

· 7 ·

MUHAMMAD

Introduction

Islam comes from the Arabic word *salaam* which means peace and submission. Islam is the peace that results by submitting oneself to God. Muslims are those who submit their lives to God. Muslims surrender to the will of God by full and faithful obedience to God's commands regarding almost every aspect of life including politics. Theology, law and politics are inseparable. Islam is an ever-growing global civilization grounded on God's commands.

Socio-political Context

The Arabian Peninsula into which Muhammad was born was populated by independent tribes; some lived in cities as merchants and bankers or on oases as agriculturists while others wandered as Bedouin herders of sheep, goats and camels. A remarkable feature of Muhammad's Arabia was its complete lack of political authority and organization. There was no central government or courts of law and each clan-based tribe was ruled by its own chief in consultation with adult male members of the tribe. Loyalty to one's tribe was primary. A common cultural code of retaliation to avenge tribal

members provided a social restraint on indiscriminate killing but also perpetuated a cycle of vindictive violence that could continue between tribes
for generations. Intertribal warfare and raids were glorified as a cultural art
as well as a valid means of gaining wealth and heroic status. Pillaging and
plundering were both a way of life and a sport. Consequently, Muhammad's
world was characterized by constant intertribal warfare, but his preaching
gradually replaced the central Arabian value of tribal loyalty with allegiance to God.

Mecca was the sacred center of worship for the myriad of Arabian tribes
who practiced animistic polytheism; each tribe worshipped personifications
of various natural forces and identified with its own ancestral deity. Arabian tribal religion revered natural phenomena and regarded them as divine
powers to be placated and petitioned. The economy of Mecca was born and
sustained in the commercialization of idol worship. People from all over the
Arabian Peninsula made seasonal pilgrimages to the holiest site in the city,
the *Kaaba*, which in Arabic means cube. *Kaaba* refers to the square-shaped
structure that enshrines the black-stone, an ancient sacred rock on which
Adam allegedly offered worship to God and where Abraham attempted to
sacrifice his son. Muhammad's clan were custodians of the *Kaaba* and *Allah*
was the God of his family. The *Kaaba* housed 360 idols, representing the
diversity of tribal affiliations with disparate deities. For their livelihood,
many merchants depended on pilgrims purchasing paraphernalia for worshipping the panoply of deities.

Caravan trade was essential to the economic life of Mecca and it served
to connect Mecca to the civilizations of Mesopotamia and the Mediterranean
world. Care and breeding of camels were basic to the Bedouin nomadic economy. Bedouins survived on camel milk-products and made a living by selling
camels and providing services for the caravans of merchants who needed protection to safely negotiate and navigate their way through marauding desert
tribes.

Texts as Context

The *Koran*, which is Arabic for read or recite, claims to be the copy of an eternal heavenly original.[1] It reveals a complete blueprint for living, covering a
wide range of topics including the Day of Judgment, resurrection of the dead,
Satan, unbelievers, obligations of the strong to care for the weak, avoidance

of idolatry, terms of divorce, inheritance, contracts, and banking regulations. It left no practical concern unaddressed.

The *Koran* is lauded as a literary miracle because, like Jesus, Muhammad had no formal education. By his own admission, he could not read. Nevertheless, the *Koran* ranks among the world's most melodious and mesmerizing masterpieces of literature. It is written in an easy to memorize rhythm and rhyme, and it is traditionally recited slowly and solemnly in a tenor and tone of sadness to convey God's great grief over the wayward. Many Muslims memorize the sacred text as children and recite it regularly throughout their lives to internalize its views and values.

The *Koran* is a collection of revelations that were received, memorized, compiled, and committed to writing over a period of 23 years. Composed of 114 chapters (*suras*) and arranged according to length from longest to shortest, the *Koran* is about the size of the Christian *New Testament*.

Birth, Youth, and Marriage

Muhammad, the founder of Islam, is an honorific title which means highly praised. We do not know his birth name. He was born into a relatively poor clan named the Hashim, who belonged to the Quraysh, a prominent merchant tribe in mid-seventh-century Mecca. Muhammad's father, Abd-Allah, died two months before he was born, and his mother, Amina, died before he reached age six. Orphaned, he was first cared for by his grandfather, Abd-al-Muttalib, who died two years later. Then Muhammad's uncle, Abu-Talib, a merchant and the new head of the Hashim clan, received custody of the young boy and trained him in the business of camel caravans. As a child, Muhammad accompanied his uncle on the annual round-trip journeys across the Arabian desert, in the winter to Syria in the north and in the summer to Yemen in the south.

As a youth, Muhammad learned to manage his own caravan. In his early 20's, he was employed by a wealthy widow named Khadijah, whose caravans he conducted and whose entire estate he managed. At age 25, Muhammad married Khadijah. Though she was 15 years older than him, their marriage was a model of mutual love, respect and support. They had three sons who died in infancy and four daughters who endured. As long as Khadijah lived, Muhammad had no other wives.

Retreat and Revelation

Throughout his marriage, Muhammad made annual pilgrimages to the hills surrounding Mecca, where he camped in caves. It was his family's tradition to go on annual spiritual retreats, during which he spent long hours in meditation contemplating nature and the wonders of the universe.

At age 40, while meditating in a cave on one such hillside retreat, Muhammad entered into a mystical trance. In a dreamlike state, he heard a majestic voice command him in his native Arabic tongue: "Read." Since Muhammad had no formal education and was illiterate, he answered the angelic voice saying: "I cannot read." Refusing to take no for an answer, the angel repeated the directive: "Read." Muhammad reiterated: "But I cannot read." Persistently the angel urged Muhammad: "Read" and pressed the pages of an open book so hard against Muhammad's mouth and nose that he nearly suffocated. Muhammad gasped:

> What can I read? The voice said: Read: In the name of the Lord who creates humanity from a clot. Read: And it is the Lord, the most bountiful who teaches by the pen, teaches people that which they do not know.[2]

When Muhammad awoke from the mystical dreamlike trance, the words he had heard were already permanently engraved on his heart. He emerged from the cave hearing the same transcendent voice say: "Oh Muhammad, you are *Allah's* messenger and I am Gabriel." Then, overlooking the hillside, Muhammad saw the angel sitting cross-legged in the form of a man on the horizon.

Standing silent and stunned, Muhammad tried to turn his gaze away from the glorious vision, but wherever he looked, the splendor of the angel continued to overwhelm him. Eventually the angel vanished, and immediately Muhammad began to question the source of his dream. He thought his vision may have been inspired by demons rather than a divine being until his wife, Khadijah, reassured and convinced Muhammad that the origin of his vision was definitely divine.

Message and Mission

Throughout the first three years after the initial revelation, Muhammad continued to receive messages mediated by the angel Gabriel. Muhammad taught them only to his immediate family and a few close friends. After those first three years, Muhammad received the revelation commanding him to preach publicly.[3]

Muhammad's public preaching was not popular. He harshly criticized the religious perspectives and practices prevalent in Mecca. Muhammad's preaching, particularly against idol worship, undermined Mecca's economy and condemned its venerated tribal ancestors to hell. The merchants of Mecca thought their 360 idols would attract far more pilgrims to their city than Muhammad's one-God-only policy.

His preaching created discord and division within families and between tribes. Throughout Mecca, Muhammad's family was the victim of an economic boycott. Were it not for the protection provided by his powerful uncle, Muhammad would certainly have been assassinated. His followers of lower socioeconomic status were not so fortunate; they were persecuted for practicing and preaching Muhammad's message. Tormented and tortured, many fled for refuge to a Christian community in Ethiopia.[4]

The Migration

At age 50, during the peak of persecution, filled with grief over the recent deaths of his beloved wife and his protector uncle, a measure of good fortune finally came to Muhammad. A delegation of tribal elders from Yathrib, a city 250 miles north of Mecca, met with Muhammad to negotiate with him to help them unify their fractured city. Rival factions in Yathrib produced political problems which they hoped Muhammad's spiritual and political prowess would solve. Over the course of the next year, about 100 Muslim families gradually migrated to Yathrib for asylum and to wait for Muhammad's arrival.

In 622, at age 52, under cover of darkness, Muhammad fled Mecca for Yathrib with his closest disciple, Abu Bakr.[5] Muhammad's midnight flight (*hegira*) to Yathrib is the pivotal moment that marks the beginning of the Muslim calendar. Were it not for the refuge offered in Yathrib, Islam may well have died with Muhammad in Mecca—but during that fateful night of flight, Muhammad received the revelation of permission from *Allah* to defend himself against the persecutors.[6] Muhammad and his followers narrowly escaped annihilation by fleeing to Yathrib, whose name later changed to Medina (the city of the Prophet).

In Medina

Muhammad resolved to settle down in Medina (formerly Yathrib) at whatever spot his camel happened to stop. There he built a clay house in which he lived a humble, rural way of life, milking his own goats and enjoying the companionship of close disciples and his nine wives. He did not sit on cushioned couches but squatted like a slave and ate no more than a slave ate. He thought of himself as the slave of God.

At that time Medina was inhabited by both Jewish and Arab tribes. The Jews were monotheists like Muhammad, and the Arabian tribal elders welcomed his role as a mediator in Medina. In that city he offered his opinion for settling disputes between factions, and he instituted new laws based on the revelations he continued to receive from *Allah*.

Medina's oasis economy was based on agriculture. Muhammad and his followers had no farming expertise or experience. In order to provide for the 100 Muslim families who had fled to Medina, Muhammad led raids on passing caravans. He also invaded Bedouin settlements with the threat of force, though he forged most of his tribal relationships through diplomacy.

The most daring of the many raids was an attack on the annual 1,000-camel caravan returning to Mecca from Syria. Having learned about Muhammad's plan to attack, the Meccans sent reinforcements to protect their caravan and to counterattack Muhammad. In a move of military genius, Muhammad positioned his troops so that the Meccans would have to attack them straight into the blinding desert sunlight. As providence predestined, a blazing sandstorm blasted the Meccans into complete retreat. Overwhelmingly outnumbered by his opponents, Muhammad's stupendous military success was testimony to many that his message and mission were valid and true.[7]

In retaliation, the Meccan tribal elders sent hundreds of soldiers on horseback to seek vengeance on Muhammad and his men. On the advice of a Persian soldier in his camp, Muhammad ordered his men to dig a ditch around the entire city. When the enemy horses reached the ditch, they could not go any farther. Frustrated and flustered, all the Meccan men and their horses retreated in defeat. By both military and diplomatic successes, Muhammad's influence grew steadily, and he consequently won the submission of polytheists, atheists and animists alike to *Allah* alone.

Conquest of Mecca

In the most triumphant of all campaigns, Muhammad led his army of Muslim patriots on a pilgrimage to worship *Allah* at the *Kaaba* in Mecca. Met with resistance by the Meccan elders, Muhammad managed to negotiate a treaty to return for a peaceful pilgrimage one year later. When Mecca broke the truce, Muhammad marched on Mecca with 10,000 soldiers and became the unchallenged and unrivaled religious and political sovereign of Mecca.

Muhammad entered the *Kaaba* and demolished all signs and symbols of polytheism enshrined there, including the 360 idols, with his bare hands; after destroying the deities he declared: "Truth has come, and falsehood has vanished."[8] Then he re-established the exclusive worship of *Allah* in the *Kaaba* and prohibited all non-Muslims from entering. However instead of staying to rule Mecca, Muhammad returned to Medina, where he continued to reign as the supreme spiritual statesman and prophet of peace.

Death and Legacy

Farewell Pilgrimage

Ten years after his migration to Medina, Muhammad made his final pilgrimage to the *Kaaba* in Mecca and recited these concluding remarks:

> Today I have completed my religion for you and fulfilled the extent of my favor towards you. It is my will that Islam be your religion. I have completed my mission. I have left you the Book of *Allah* and clear commandments. If you keep them, you will never go wrong.[9]

Only three months later in Medina, complaining of a severe headache, Muhammad expired unexpectedly at his mosque-house under the care of his favorite wife, Aisha. As he lay dying, he declared:

> No one has the right to be worshipped except *Allah*. Death has its agonies. He then lifted his hands toward the heavens and went on repeating, "With the highest companion," until he dropped his hands and expelled his final breath.[10]

Upon receiving news of Muhammad's death, his disciples refused to believe it, insisting that he must be immortal and could not die. In a community crisis of faith, Muhammad's closest disciple, Abu Bakr, stepped forward and declared: "If it is Muhammad that you worship, know that he is dead. If it is God that you worship, know that he is alive and lives forever."[11]

In the aftermath of Muhammad's unanticipated death, the community split over the question of the Prophet's successor. The controversy still defines and demarcates the two major divisions of Islam even today. Nevertheless, by the time of Muhammad's death, the empire of Islam had transformed most of Arabia from a polytheistic, cruel culture of blood feuds, debauchery and lawlessness into a new civilization of radically moral monotheists united by the faith that there is no God but *Allah* and Muhammad is his Messenger.

Teachings

The Five Pillars

While in Medina, Muhammad continued to receive revelations which established the foundational practices that define the Islamic way of life. Submission to God is comprehensive, encompassing every aspect of private and public life. It draws no lines between the secular and sacred; there is no separation of politics from piety. Submission to *Allah* is expressed especially through practicing the five pillars: creed, prayer, fasting, charity and pilgrimage.

The Creed. The first pillar is the gateway to becoming a Muslim. Anyone can become a Muslim by simply and sincerely confessing the creed: "There is no God but *Allah* and Muhammad is his Messenger." These are the very first words pious Muslim parents whisper into the ears of their newborn children. Devout Muslims repeat the creed countless times throughout their lives both privately and publicly, as well as silently and aloud.

Allah is the Arabic term for God. *Al* is the definite article: it simply means "the," *Ilia* is the generic term for God, combined they spell *Allah*, literally "the God." In Muhammad's day, *Allah* referred specifically to the creator God, the principal proprietor who presides over the *Kaaba*. *Allah* was the God of Muhammad's clan, who were custodians of the *Kaaba*.

Muhammad insists that *Allah* cannot be represented in any way, shape or form, but the *Koran* reveals the divine attributes of *Allah*. All but one chapter of the *Koran* begin with the words: "*Allah*, the compassionate, the merciful." *Allah* is the one and only all-powerful, all-knowing, sovereign ruler of the universe. Above and beyond all that can be thought or imagined, *Allah* is utterly transcendent and has no equal, no rival, no partner, no parents, no daughters or sons.[12]

According to Muhammad, *Allah* is the God whom Adam worshipped in the Garden of Eden. *Allah* is the God of Abraham to whom Islam traces its origin through Ishmael, the first-born son of Abraham and Hagar. Muhammad taught that Abraham attempted to sacrifice his son Ishmael (not Isaac as the Hebrew Bible reports). According to Muhammad, the attempted sacrifice took place on the black-rock enshrined at the center of the *Kaaba*.

To profess that Muhammad is the Messenger of *Allah* is to declare Muhammad to be the seal of the prophets, the final authoritative word from God. According to Muhammad, the messages of previous prophets—like Adam, Abraham, Moses, Jonah and Jesus—were only partial and incomplete; they were each intended for a particular people, period and place. But Muhammad's message, he insisted, is the full and final word from God for everybody, everywhere, always.

Moreover, Muhammad taught that the scriptures of Judaism and Christianity have been compromised. The revelation received by Muhammad in the *Koran* fulfilled the law and spirit of previous prophets and corrected their corrupted scriptures. To profess that Muhammad is *Allah's* Messenger is to proclaim that his message and mission supersede all those who came before.

Prayer. The second pillar of Islamic practice is prayer.[13] The principle purpose of periodic prayer is to remind human beings that they are not God but dependent creatures.

Prayer puts people in their place. Prostration in prayer is a bodily expression of submission. Not merely lip service, Islamic prayer involves the whole person—body, mind and spirit. It is not informal but intimate, not randomly recited but punctually performed.

While many Muslims practice perpetual prayer, all Muslims are to perform prescribed worship five times each day—at sunrise, noon, mid-afternoon, sunset and mid-evening. In common practice, the form and content of prayer varies. One of the most frequently repeated prayers is found in the very first chapter of the *Koran*.

> Praise be to God, Lord of the universe, the compassionate, the merciful, sovereign of the Day of Judgment. You alone we worship and to you alone we turn for help. Guide us to the straight path, the path of those whom you have favored, not of those who have incurred your wrath, nor of those who have gone astray.[14]

The Muslim can pray anywhere because the whole earth is sacred, and a portable prayer rug sanctifies any spot for worship. Muslims pray facing Mecca—standing, bowing, kneeling and prostrating themselves toward the

Kaaba, the altar of *Allah*.[15] In many Muslim majority cultures, public address systems melodiously call people to public and private prayer. Five times a day, Muslims suspend whatever they are doing to face and encounter the intimate presence of God, after which they resume their uninterrupted mission of subservience and submission in everything to *Allah*. The *Koran* commands: "When your prayers are ended, remember God whether you are standing, sitting or lying down."[16]

Fasting. The third pillar is fasting.[17] Its primary purpose is to cultivate empathetic compassion for all who struggle in hunger and starvation. Hunger is the plight and predicament of populations all over the world. Feeling hunger by fasting is calculated to make Muslims sensitive to the needs of others. Fasting is also a spiritual discipline designed to develop self-control by cultivating patience and perseverance in the face of daily deprivations and difficulties.

Throughout one particular month of each lunar year, Muslims everywhere unite in their daily discipline of deprivation, refraining from food, drink and sex during daylight hours. The fast is undertaken during the Muslim month called *Ramadan*. It is the month in which Muhammad received his first revelation; it is also the month of Muhammad's migration from Mecca to Medina. For these momentous reasons, *Ramadan* was made the month for Muslims to fast.

Charity. The fourth pillar is charity.[18] In Medina, Muhammad implemented a charity tax to provide for the widows, orphans and vulnerable members of society. The harsh and hostile Bedouin culture cared little for the unfortunate and often exploited the weak and helpless for their own gain. To redress this systemic social injustice, Muhammad enjoined all Muslims to contribute two and one-half percent of their total wealth annually. Muhammad did not leave charity to chance. He legislated love by instituting a tax to take care of the poor. This tax is not for the maintenance of mosques or Muslim administrators or ministers; it is social welfare for those in need of basic goods and services. The *Koran* commands committed, concerned care for the unfortunate more than anything other than the exclusive worship of God.

Pilgrimage. The fifth pillar is the pilgrimage (*hajj*).[19] It is enjoined upon all Muslims who are able to make a once in a lifetime journey to Mecca to worship in the sacred center of Islam. Mecca is the birthplace of Muhammad, where he received the first revelations, and Mecca is the home of the *Kaaba*, the original shrine and ancient altar of *Allah*.

Muhammad's final pilgrimage provided the pattern and example for future Muslims to follow. Upon approaching the sacred city, pilgrims change into identical seamless, white burial robes that symbolize their solidarity in submission and their equality under *Allah*. The pilgrims proceed by foot to the *Kaaba*, which they circumambulate seven times while incessantly reciting: "There is no God but *Allah*." With intense fervor, the faithful feel the presence of *Allah* and experience the unity of an international global community.

The pilgrims then proceed to a sacred plot of land on which Adam and Eve allegedly received the revelation that humans were created to worship God. From noon until sunset, pilgrims pray for the forgiveness of sins; they also throw stones at pillars that symbolize Satan and ritually slaughter animals to commemorate Abraham's sacrifice of a ram instead of his son, Ishmael.

In another part of the pilgrimage, Muslims re-enact the plight of Ishmael's mother, Hagar, who ran frantically between two hills in search of water to save herself and her son from dying of thirst. This custom commemorates the miraculous moment when God caused a well to spring up for the salvation of Hagar, and Ishmael, the founding father of Muhammad's family.[20] The pilgrimage culminates in final circumambulations around the *Kaaba* before the faithful return home with new designations prefixed to their names (Al-Haji) to indicate their fulfillment of the final pillar.

Jihad

Jihad is not a pillar of Islam. Muhammad divided the world into two abodes: the abode of submission, encompassing Islamic territories, and the abode of struggle, which includes all non-Islamic lands. The Medieval aim of *jihad* (holy struggle) was to expand the abode of submission through missionary, and, if necessary, military campaigns. The goal of *jihad* was to gain peaceful political control over societies and govern them by the principles of Islam. Today, the vast majority of Muslims world-wide denounce the doctrine as Medieval, antiquated and antithetical to the true message and universal mission of Islam. So-called "radical Islamic terrorists" do not reflect the letter or spirit of Muhammad's military philosophy or spiritual strategy, and they are as much a menace to Muslims as they are to everyone else.

Muhammad encouraged Muslims to engage in the greater *jihad* of the heart, an inner spiritual struggle against base impulses and idolatry, which he regarded as far more important than any military campaign of conquest or expansion.

Between Muhammad and Jesus

Some scholars of religion suggest that when comparing Christianity and Islam, Jesus should not be likened to Muhammad but to the *Koran* since Christianity claims God is revealed primarily in a person, whereas Islam stresses that God is revealed principally in a book. However, it is appropriate to compare Muhammad to Jesus because they both founded forms of monotheism. Moreover, the disclosure of God in Jesus is revealed in the Bible just as the message of *Allah* is mediated by Gabriel through Muhammad in the *Koran*.

Jesus and Muhammad were like-minded in understanding their missions as servants of God. They saw themselves as heirs to traditions which preceded them. Just as Jesus claimed that he came to fulfill the law and the prophets, Muhammad understood his mission as a revolution to return Arabians to the radical monotheism of Abraham.

Muhammad and Jesus both performed prophetic roles and spoke truth to power. Just as Jesus challenged and chastised the Jewish religious authorities, likewise Muhammad confronted and condemned the Arabian ruling elite, including members of his own family. The same prophetic impulse and religious rage which compelled Jesus to turn over the tables and chase the currency exchangers out of the temple in Jerusalem also drove Muhammad to demolish the idols inside the *Kaaba* in Mecca. Jesus, no less than Muhammad, warned his audiences of the inevitable, impending day of God's judgment. Jesus threatened condemnation and hell to the unrepentant as often as Muhammad promised peace and paradise to the righteous.

Muhammad, like Jesus, was a victim of ridicule, rejection and persecution. Muhammad, no less than Jesus, declared God's eagerness to forgive everyone of almost everything. But whereas Muhammad received a revelation from *Allah* permitting him to defend himself and pursue persecutors until all opposition was eradicated, Jesus taught his disciples to love their enemies and pray for those who persecuted them. Armed with the threat of *Allah's* righteous vengeance, Muhammad bartered peace in exchange for submission while resisters and rebels paid the price with expulsions and executions.

Muhammad was the merchant of Mecca who peddled peace, a commodity as rare in his day as it is today. Peace is precious because it comes at a high price. Muhammad preferred negotiations to military conquest and spread his revelations primarily through peaceful diplomacy rather than by his sword.[21] When asked how best to practice Islam, Muhammad directed people to feed the hungry and spread peace among those you know as well as those you don't.

Muhammad was a man of deep humility who confessed that he prayed for forgiveness 70 times each day. He did not presume to be perfect. He was not a broker of God's forgiveness. Standing in need of forgiveness himself, Muhammad was in no position to mediate it to anyone else.

Jesus, by contrast, claimed to have divine authority to forgive sin. Jesus is the prince of peace. In a farewell speech to his disciples, Jesus said: "My peace I leave you, my peace I give you; I do not give to you as the world gives."[22] The peace of which Jesus speaks is not gained on the basis of obedient submission—rather it is granted as a gift from God who freely forgives. The peace is not the consequence of unconditional surrender to God; it is the result of unconditional love from God. The peace that Jesus gives is not based on obedience but on faith in God's promise of forgiveness. "These things I have told you so that in me you may have peace; in the world you will have trouble, but I have overcome the world."[23]

What Christians Might Learn From Muhammad

From Muhammad, Christians might learn the priority of prayer. Muhammad made a habit of prayer. He understood that humans are habitual creatures whose characters and personalities are shaped by repeated patterns of behavior. Capitalizing on this insight into human nature, Muhammad prescribed prayer in regularly scheduled daily doses. He routinized the ritual of worship. Muhammad prioritized prayer by punctuating and permeating each day with its practice. For Muhammad worship was not only a way of life—it was the principal purpose of life itself. Muhammad was a prayer warrior which he practiced as a spiritual science.

Prayer requires a disposition of dependence. It reminds people of what they are most prone to forget—that they are utterly and entirely dependent on the will and grace of God. By demarcating and pervading the day with prayer, Christians can develop a disposition of dependence on God and experience God's presence. People make time for activities they deem important. Purposeful periods of prayer, like any important activity, require disciplined scheduling. Establishing set times throughout the day to suspend whatever one is doing to worship God is one way to prioritize prayer as a pillar for the practice of faith. Nevertheless, whether a person prays five times per day or perpetually, prayer is communion with God which is the primary purpose of life.

Notes

1. *Koran* 85:22, translated by Pickthall, Mohammed Marmaduke, *The Meaning of the Glorious Koran: An Explanatory Translation*, Meridian, May 1997. All references to the *Koran* are based on this translation unless otherwise noted.
2. *Koran* 96:1–5.
3. *Koran* 74:2.
4. *Koran* 19.
5. *Koran* 9:40.
6. *Koran* 8:39.
7. *Koran* 8.
8. *Koran* 17:81.
9. *Koran* 5:3.
10. *Hadith: Sahih al-Bukhari*, 5:736, translated by Muhammad M. Khan, Dar-us-Salam Publications, 1997.
11. *Hadith: Sahih al-Bukhari*, 5:736.
12. *Koran* 17:111.
13. *Koran* 2:238.
14. *Koran* 1:1–7.
15. *Koran* 2:144.
16. *Koran* 4:103.
17. *Koran* 2:183–187.
18. *Koran* 2:110; 9:103.
19. *Koran* 3:97.
20. *Genesis* 21:14–21, *Holy Bible: New International Version*, Zondervan Publishers, 1984. All Bible references are based on this translation unless otherwise noted.
21. *Koran* 2:16.
22. *John* 14:27.
23. *John* 16:33.

· 8 ·

JESUS

Introduction

There are wide-ranging opinions about who Jesus was. Members of his own family thought he had gone mad.[1] Some priests and rabbis claimed Jesus was demon-possessed.[2] Herod, the Roman governor of the district where Jesus roamed, heard he might be a rebel rouser and revolutionary threat to the peace and order of his jurisdiction of the empire. His disciples believed he was the *Messiah*, though they initially misunderstood the nature and destiny of the role he came to fulfill.

Socio-political Context

The life and teaching of Jesus can be understood against the background of Roman imperial rule.[3] Jesus was born in the reign of Octavian, who rose to power during a period of civil wars following the assassination of Julius Caesar, who was deified upon death. Caesar's adopted son and heir, Octavian, was given the title of Augustus (one to be revered) since he was lauded as the Son of God and Savior of the world for establishing the *Pax Romana*, a glorious age of Roman peace and prosperity. However, the peace was procured and maintained by military force, and the prosperity was purchased at the price of heavy taxation on the vast majority of the Empire's agrarian peasant population. Augustus created the appearance of peace and prosperity that benefited the elite members of society most: senators, soldiers and citizens living inside the city of Rome itself, though people in general did see benefits during his reign in the form of roads, amphitheaters, aqueducts, baths and other public projects. His welfare program of free bread and entertainment was a policy that kept the privileged populace fed and entertained at the unbearable expense of economically impoverished and politically oppressed people throughout the entire empire.

The region in which Jesus lived and taught, Galilee, was politically subjugated and economically oppressed by Roman imperial rule. Members of the Herodian family were appointed as client-kings by Augustus to rule the region of Judea and Galilee. Jewish reactions to Roman rule ranged from compliance, cooperation and collusion to nonconformity, peaceful protest and armed rebellion.

Consequently, the people of Israel longed for a *Messianic* king to deliver them from the hands of their harsh oppressors and to lead them into a glorious new age of God's universal reign on earth. The word *Messiah* is Hebrew for anointed one; *Christ* is its Greek translation. Different factions within Judaism held varying versions and visions of expectations regarding the *Messiah*. A mix of *Messianic* images complicated the matter of recognizing him whenever he happened to arrive. Some anticipated that the *Messiah* would be a military man who would lead an insurrection and overthrow Rome in an armed assault; others expected the *Messiah* would be a mystical man who would spectacularly appear, descending from the clouds of heaven. His disciples drew from the mixture of metaphors to identify Jesus as the long-awaited *Messiah*, savior of the world. The kingdom that Jesus announced and inaugurated was in opposition to the Roman Empire. The kingdom of God subverts and supplants all kingdoms of the world.[4] In the context of oppressive Roman rule, Jesus said: "Take my yoke upon you and learn from me, for my yoke is easy and my load is light."[5]

Texts as Context

The primary source for the life and teachings of Jesus are the *Gospels*, the first four books of the *New Testament*. Though Jesus probably spoke Aramaic and perhaps Hebrew, his life and teachings are recorded in Greek, the common, commercial language of the Mediterranean world. The word *gospel* is a translation of the Greek word *euangelion*. News and political propaganda about the deeds of Augustus were announced publicly and introduced as the *euangelion*, Greek for good news. The *Gospels* of *Matthew*, *Mark*, *Luke* and *John* boldly proclaim the *euangelion* of Jesus, and present him as the Son of God and Savior of the world, rivaling and challenging the claim of Augustus and subsequent Caesars.[6]

Text-historical scholars differ regarding the dating of the *Gospels* but general scholarly consensus situates their composition within the first century. Biblical scholars who differentiate between a historical Jesus and a Christ of faith tend to assign later dates to the *Gospels*, but traditionalists favor the view of the early church fathers.

Accordingly, the *Gospel of Mark* was composed by John Mark, Peter's companion and interpreter during his missionary journeys. Mark wrote from Rome to help encourage Christians to face the impending persecutions of Emperor Nero. One of Mark's central themes is the secrecy of Jesus' *Messianic* identity. In the first half of Mark's *Gospel*, Jesus neither reveals nor admits that he is the *Messiah*. Only after Peter proclaims him to be the *Messiah* does Jesus affirm the truth, but he warns his disciples to tell no one. Since *Mark* is the oldest and shortest *Gospel*, we will trace the biography of Jesus by following its outline.

The Gospel of Matthew was written by Matthew, also called Levi, a tax collector and one of the original 12 disciples appointed by Jesus. He composed his *Gospel* to persuade a Jewish audience that Jesus is their long-awaited *Messiah*. He presents Jesus as the new Moses, who leads a new exodus from sin into a new covenant cut in his own blood.

Matthew focuses on Jesus' fulfillment of prophecy, which he proves by quoting over 60 passages from the Greek translation of the *Old Testament*. His *Gospel* begins by introducing Jesus as Immanuel, which means God with us, and concludes with Jesus assuring his disciples that he will be with them always, even to the end of the age. The mission of Matthew's *Gospel* was to overcome the bias, prejudice and skepticism of its original audience and demonstrate that Jesus is their long-awaited *Messianic* king.

The Gospel of Luke was composed by Luke, a medical doctor and historian, who accompanied the apostle Paul during periods of his missionary journeys. Luke announces the purpose of his *Gospel* in its prologue: so that Theophilus (lover of God) may know the certainty about the things that have been taught regarding Jesus.[7]

The *Gospel of John* was composed by John, the beloved disciple of Jesus. He clearly states his reason for writing: "These things are written that you may believe that Jesus is the *Messiah*, the Son of God, and that by believing you may have life in his name."[8]

Backstory, Birth, and Youth

Jesus was conceived and born in the shadow of sexual scandal. The *Gospel of Matthew* begins with a genealogy to address the rumor of illegitimacy regarding the birth of Jesus and to demonstrate that he is the *Messiah* who comes from a lineage of sexually illicit relationships. He exposes that Jesus is not only a direct descendant of Abraham, Isaac, Jacob and David—but also of Tamar, Rahab, Ruth and Bathsheba.[9] Ancient Near Eastern genealogies did not include women; Matthew's ancestral account of Jesus is the only one that does. He interrupts the familiar "so-and-so was the father of so-and-so" by interjecting the refrain: "whose mother was so-and-so." *Matthew* refers to four mothers besides Mary.

First is Tamar, who impersonated a prostitute to lure her father-in-law, Judah, into sleeping with her. Thus, she became pregnant with an ancestor of the *Messiah*. Second is Rahab, the prostitute from Jericho who harbored the Israeli spies in order to aid and abet the Israelites in conquering the city. She married an Israeli soldier and took her privileged place as a foremother of the *Messiah*. Third is Ruth, a woman from Moab, the nation named after the son of Lot's daughter, who got her father drunk with wine in order to conceive his child. The Hebrew Bible records how Ruth, who harvested in the fields of a Jewish bachelor named Boaz, entered his home one evening and slept at his feet, an ancient Near Eastern ritual to symbolize sexual submission and marriage proposal.[10] Accordingly, she married Boaz and took her pedigreed place in the long line of the *Messiah's* scandalously suspect forbearers. Fourth is Bathsheba, referred to as the wife of Uriah the Hittite, who was a soldier in king David's army. David committed adultery with Bathsheba, got her pregnant and arranged to have her husband killed so that he could marry her. Bathsheba's child was stillborn, but she subsequently gave birth to Solomon, who became king of Israel. Like Solomon, Jesus was called the Son of David and king of Israel, one of the many designations for the Jewish *Messiah*.

In ancient Israel sexual scandal could cost a person their life, specifically if found guilty of homosexuality, lesbianism, incest, bestiality or adultery. When Joseph first learned that his fiancé Mary was pregnant, he privately planned to divorce her and hide her away from those who would want to stone her to death for adultery. Before he could act, God dispatched the angel Gabriel to inform Joseph that the scandal was part of God's plan to redeem people from their sin. Gabriel appeared to Joseph in a dream to assure him that Mary's pregnancy was sanctioned and sanctified by God.[11]

Matthew's narrative of Christ's birth reveals that he was not invited into the world but descended in the indecency, inconvenience, imposition and intrusion of an unintended pregnancy. *Matthew* presents the *Messianic* king as the bastard son of a sexually suspect teenage girl—but also the Son of David and the Son of God. He neither affirms nor denies the slanderous rumor of illegitimacy; instead *Matthew* presents the mother of Jesus as one among a whole ancestry of questionable women. The miracle of Jesus' birth was not the virtuous virginity of Mary as his mother but the divine identity of God as his heavenly Father.[12]

Accordingly, Gabriel told Mary to name her son Jesus because he came to save his people from their sin. Entering the world under the shadow and shame of sexual sin, Jesus came to be despised, disrespected, ridiculed and rejected. God's *Messiah* entered the world in sexual scandal, contrary to popular pious expectations.

Apart from one incident related by the *Gospel* writers, we know next to nothing about Jesus' childhood, youth or early adult life. At age 12, his family took their annual pilgrimage to Jerusalem for the Passover festival. Jesus disappeared into the temple courts where the young boy astounded the rabbis, priests and legal scholars with his knowledge of the scriptures.[13]

During the trip home in a long caravan of relatives, his parents did not realize that Jesus had been left behind. When his parents discovered his absence, they frantically returned to Jerusalem to find him talking with priests in the temple.

> When his parents saw him, they were astonished. His mother said to him: "Son, why have you treated us like this? Your father and I have been anxiously searching for you." "Why were you searching for me," Jesus asked? "Didn't you know I had to be in my father's house?"[14]

The *Gospel of Luke* reports that from that time forward Jesus grew in wisdom and stature with God and men—but no further details are divulged until age 30, when he appears in the wilderness to be baptized by his cousin John the Baptist.

In the absence of any recorded activity during his teenage and early adult years, some have claimed that Jesus traveled to India during that period.[15] There he allegedly spent the intervening years at the feet of yogis, learning spiritual wisdom, and the healing arts, such as how to walk on water and how to perform other paranormal powers. Fanciful theories notwithstanding, there is no credible or compelling evidence that Jesus ever traveled or trained in India.

Jewish fathers are responsible for training their children to use two body parts: the mind with which to study the law of God, and the thumb with which to earn a living. Jesus applied his mind to the study of the Hebrew scriptures, in which he may have discovered his *Messianic* identity and mission. As the step-son of a carpenter, Jesus likely labored as a craftsman and lived in a lower-class extended family household. He interacted and negotiated daily life with parents, brothers, sisters, uncles, aunts, cousins, customers and friends. Jesus probably never traveled more than 50 miles from home throughout his relatively short life.

Baptism and Renunciation

Around the age when most Jewish men enter marriage, Jesus initiated his *Messianic* mission by submitting himself to a public baptism. The *Gospel of Mark* begins by identifying Jesus as the *Messiah*, Son of God, and John the Baptist as the harbinger of the *Messiah*, about whom the prophet predicted: "I will send my messenger ahead of you who will prepare your way—a voice of one crying in the wilderness, prepare the way of the Lord, make paths straight for him."[16]

After baptizing Jesus, John witnessed the skies opening up, a dove descending upon Jesus, and a voice from above declaring: "This is my son, whom I love, with whom I am well-pleased."[17] Jesus inaugurated his mission with a public prophetic testimony to his identity as the *Messiah* and his mission as the lamb of God who takes away the sins of the world. John the Baptist is the final prophet of the old covenant and harbinger of the *Messiah* who introduces a new covenant. *The Gospel of Luke* explains how John the Baptist demarcates the end of an old era and the beginning of a new age: "The law and the prophets were proclaimed until John. Since that time the good news of the kingdom of God is being preached and everyone is forcing their way into it."[18]

Immediately after the baptism, Jesus was swept away by the spirit to the desert to pray and prepare for his mission and to be tested by Satan. During a 40-day preparatory period of fasting and prayer, Jesus successfully defeated Satan's design to derail his divine mission.[19]

After renouncing Satan by resisting all attempts to pre-empt his purpose, Jesus returned home. Only upon learning that John the Baptist had been arrested and thrown into prison did Jesus go to the lake region of Galilee and begin to preach the good news of the kingdom of God: "The time has come; the kingdom of God has come near. Repent and believe the good news!"[20] Repent means to change one's mind by turning toward God and away from sin; believe means to have faith—a disposition of trust and dependence on God; the good news to be believed is that the kingdom of God has arrived.

Message, Mission, and Ministry

The message, mission and ministry of Jesus are inseparable. His purpose is inextricably bound up in his personal identity as the *Messianic* king. For three years, Jesus traveled around Palestine gathering followers and teaching them the nature and destiny of the kingdom of God in parables that were paradoxical, puzzling and difficult to interpret. Jesus told his disciples:

> The secret of the kingdom of God has been given to you. But to those outside everything is said in parables so that they may be ever seeing but never perceiving and ever hearing but never understanding; otherwise they might turn and be forgiven.[21]

From the humble ranks of humanity, Jesus gathered and trained potential leaders to attract and cultivate citizens for the kingdom of God. His first four followers were fishermen, including two sets of brothers among whom Peter, James and John became the most beloved and devoted disciples. Drawing on their career as a metaphor for his mission, Jesus said to them: "Come, follow me and I will send you out to fish for people."[22]

The *Gospel of Mark* describes how Jesus and his four followers went first to Capernaum, entered a synagogue on the sabbath, and began to teach. The people were amazed at the authority with which Jesus taught. While Jesus was teaching them, a man possessed by a demon disrupted the assembly by shouting: "What do you want with us, Jesus? Have you come to destroy us? I know who you are—the Holy one of God." Jesus responded sternly: "Be quiet; come out of him." [23] The demon came out with a shriek and all who witnessed it were amazed with the new teaching and authority of Jesus. News about him spread rapidly throughout the region of Galilee.

As soon as Jesus and his four followers left the synagogue, they went immediately to the home of Peter and Andrew, where they found Peter's mother-in-law sick in bed with a fever. Jesus went to her, took her by the hand, and helped her up. The fever left her and she began to wait on them.[24] That same evening people brought all the demon-possessed and sick to Jesus, who healed various diseases and cast out demons but would not let the demons speak because they knew who he was.[25]

The next morning Jesus rose early and went off to a solitary place to pray. When his disciples found him, they informed him that people were clamoring for him, but Jesus replied: "Let us go somewhere else—to the nearby villages—so I can preach there also. That is why I have come."[26] He went around preaching and casting out demons. He healed a leper and told him to tell no one—but the leper spread the news, and consequently Jesus could not enter into any city due to his notoriety and popularity. From that moment on he stayed outside cities in isolated places, but crowds came to him from everywhere.

The fifth disciple Jesus called was Levi. He was a tax-collector working on behalf of the Roman government and was regarded as ritually unclean by the religious establishment of Jerusalem. When criticized for associating with tax-collectors and questionable characters, Jesus retorted: "It is not the healthy who need a doctor but the sick. I have not come to call the righteous but sinners."[27]

Soon thereafter, Jesus ascended a mountain slope and selected 12 disciples and called them to himself. He appointed them to be with him, sent them out to preach, and gave them authority to drive out demons. He warned the unclean spirits not to tell anyone that he is the Son of God. Wherever he went, people cried out for healing. He raised from the dead the daughter of a leading local synagogue official and told them to tell no one about it. He cured a deaf mute and told him to tell no one, but the more Jesus insisted on keeping his identity secret, the more the people publicized it. While alone with his disciples, Jesus asked them: "Who do people say I am?" After reporting diverse popular opinions, Peter confessed: "You are the *Messiah*, the Son of the living God." Jesus commanded him to tell no one.[28]

One might well wonder why Jesus wanted to keep his identity secret and hidden from the public. The *Gospel of John* provides an explanation. After miraculously feeding 5,000 people, the people began to say: "Surely this is the prophet who has come into the world. Jesus, knowing that they intended to come and make him king by force, withdrew again to a mountain by himself."[29]

Jesus taught his disciples that he must suffer and be rejected by elders, chief priests and teachers of the law, and that he must be killed and after three days rise again.[30] Peter particularly protested but Jesus rebuked him for failing to understand the purpose and plan of God and spelled out the requirements for discipleship. "Then he called the crowd and his disciples to himself and said: Whoever wants to be my disciple must deny themselves, take up their cross and follow me."[31]

Jesus took Peter, James and John aside and led them to the top of a hill, where he transfigured himself into a radiant revelation of divinity and appeared between Moses and Elijah, representing the Law and the Prophets respectively. Peter was so dumbfounded that he did not know what to do but offered to set up tents for each of them. Immediately a cloud enveloped Jesus, Moses and Elijah, and the disciples heard a voice coming from the cloud: "This is my Son, with whom I am pleased. Listen to him."[32] When the cloud cleared, only Jesus remained. He told his disciples: "Don't tell anyone what you saw until after I have risen from the dead."[33] But the disciples had no idea what he was talking about and discussed among themselves what "rising from the dead" might mean; they did not understand his mission despite having been told repeatedly. Again Jesus told his disciples: "The Son of Man is going to be delivered into the hands of men. They will kill him and after three days, he will rise." But they didn't understand and were afraid to ask him about it.[34]

As they moved through Galilee, the disciples argued about who among themselves was the greatest. Knowing what they were quarrelling about, Jesus sat down and called the 12 disciples to himself and said: "Anyone who wants to be first must be the very last, the servant of all."[35]

While they were on their way to Jerusalem, Jesus took the 12 disciples aside again and told them what was going to happen to him: "We are going up to Jerusalem and the Son of Man will be delivered over to the chief priests and teachers of the law. They will condemn him to death and hand him over to the Gentiles, who will mock him and spit on him, flog him and kill him. Three days later he will rise."[36]

While on the way to Jerusalem, James and John asked Jesus for the special honor of sitting at his right and left when he ascends the throne in his kingdom. When the other disciples heard about it, they became indignant, but Jesus called them together and set them straight about the radically different kind of kingdom and kingship his would be:

> You know that those who are regarded as rulers of the Gentiles lord it over them, and their high officials exercise authority over them. Not so with you. Instead, whoever wants to become great among you, must be your servant, and whoever wants to be first, must be slave of all. For even the Son of Man did not come to be served but to serve and give his life as ransom for many.[37]

Jesus arranged with his disciples to enter into Jerusalem with the pomp and procession of a king's parade, riding on a colt and welcomed by throngs of people crowding the roadside and proclaiming: "Hosanna, blessed is he who comes in the name of the Lord. Blessed is the coming kingdom of our father David. Hosanna in the highest heaven!"[38] The religious establishment began looking for an opportunity to kill him, for they feared him because the crowd was amazed at his teaching.[39] As the Passover holiday approached, the chief priests and teachers of the law were scheming to arrest Jesus and have him killed but "not during the festival," they said, "or the people will riot."[40] During the Passover meal, Jesus introduced a new covenant cut and sealed by his own body and blood.

> While they were eating, Jesus took the bread, and when he had given thanks, he broke it and gave it to his disciples, saying, "Take it; this is my body." Then he took a cup and when he had given thanks, he gave it to them and they all drank from it. "This is my blood of the covenant, which is poured out for many," he said to them.[41]

One of the 12 disciples, Judas Iscariot, conspired with the chief priests to betray Jesus. After eating the Passover meal and singing a hymn, Jesus and his disciples withdrew to the garden of Gethsemane. There, Jesus instructed his disciples to keep watch while he prayed in solitude, but they all fell asleep and did not notice the approach of Judas Iscariot, escorting a crowd of men with weapons to arrest him. Jesus woke them: "Are you still sleeping and resting? Enough! The hour has come. Look, the Son of Man is delivered into the hands of sinners. Arise! Let us go! Here comes my betrayer."[42] When the crowd arrived to arrest him, Jesus said:

Am I leading a rebellion that you have come out with swords and clubs to capture me? Every day I was with you, teaching in the temple courts, and you did not arrest me. But the Scriptures must be fulfilled.[43]

Jesus was arrested and brought before the Sanhedrin, the religious ruling authorities of Jerusalem. They were searching for evidence and testimony that would sentence Jesus to death but the contradictory, false witnesses failed to establish a credible case against him. The high priest pressed Jesus: "Are you the *Messiah*, the Son of the Blessed One?" Jesus answered: "I am and you will see the Son of Man sitting at the right hand of the Mighty One and coming on the clouds of heaven." The high priest condemned Jesus of blasphemy and they all declared him worthy of death. Then some began to spit at him; they blindfolded him, struck him with their fists, and the guards took him and beat him.[44] The next day they took Jesus to Pilate, the governor of Judaea, who asked him: "Are you the king of the Jews?" Jesus replied: "You have said so." Despite finding no justifiable basis for execution, in order to politically please the agitated crowd clamoring to kill him, Pilate had Jesus flogged and handed over to be crucified.[45]

Death and Resurrection

The soldiers led Jesus away, put a purple robe on him, then twisted together a crown of thorns and set it on his head. After mocking and hailing him as King of the Jews, they struck him in the head with a staff, spit on him, replaced the robe with his own clothes and led him out to be crucified.[46]

It was nine o'clock in the morning when they crucified him. The written notice of the charge against him read: THE KING OF THE JEWS.[47] By three o'clock in the afternoon Jesus cried out: "My God, my God, why have you forsaken me?" And with a loud cry Jesus breathed his last. When Pilate learned that Jesus was dead, he released the body to Joseph of Arimathea, an admirer of Jesus and prominent member of the Sanhedrin, who took it down from the cross, washed it, wrapped it in linen cloth, placed it in a tomb cut out of rock and rolled a stone against its entrance.[48]

The oldest extant *Gospel of Mark* ends abruptly with two female disciples of Jesus returning to his tomb only to find it open and empty. As they entered the tomb, they were shocked to see a young man seated in a white robe who addressed them:

> Don't be alarmed. You are looking for Jesus, the Nazarene, who was crucified. He
> has risen! He is not here. See the place where they laid him. But go tell his disciples
> and Peter that he is going ahead of you to Galilee. There you will see him just as he
> told you.[49]

The *Gospels of Matthew, Luke and John* report eye witnesses of the risen Jesus, who appeared repeatedly to his disciples over a period of 40 days. The women witnesses went to the group of disciples who were hiding in an upper room for fear of being identified and prosecuted as associates of Jesus. At first, none of the disciples believed their report, but then Peter and John ran to the tomb and found it empty. The disciples moved on from there to meet with others in Jerusalem, where Jesus appeared and reprimanded them for not believing the women's prior report. He reminded them how he had taught them that the *Messiah* must suffer and die, but that God would raise him from the dead on the third day.

Before departing, Jesus spoke these final words to his disciples: "Go into all the world and preach the gospel to all creation. Whoever believes will be saved, but whoever does not believe will be condemned."[50] After speaking to them, he was taken up into heaven and sat at the right hand of God.

Teachings

The Kingdom of God

In Jesus' day the kingdom of God was regarded as a future, supernatural kingdom that would bring history to a close and usher in a new world for God's redeemed people. Jesus neither challenged nor contradicted this view but taught that his *Messianic* ministry inaugurated the arrival of the kingdom of God, which is now partially present on earth though not yet completely culminated. The kingdom was inaugurated in Jesus' words and procured by his deeds, death and resurrection but its consummation remains in the future.

The kingdom refers to the authority and rule of God. Its source of sovereignty does not derive from military might or popular appeal but from God, who has authorized Jesus to rule.

> My kingdom is not of this world. If my kingdom were of this world, my servants would
> have been fighting, that I might not be delivered over to die. But my kingdom is

not of this world. For this purpose I was born, and for this purpose I have come into the world—to bear witness to the truth. Everyone who is of the truth listens to my voice.[51]

The kingdom is conceived and constructed by God; it is inherited and received, not earned or achieved. It is a divine—not human—accomplishment. The parables regarding the kingdom of God reveal the secret that Jesus is its king who demands hearers to make a personal decision to accept or reject his *Messianic* rule.

Between Jesus and the Giants

While we have observed striking similarities, the distinguishing difference between Jesus and other foundational religious figures is a question of identities and missions. How did each giant understand himself and his mission?

Muhammad understood himself to be the final Messenger of God. He believed that his message of salvation by submission to God superseded the teachings of previous prophets and fulfilled the unfinished business of Jesus.

Moses described himself as slow of speech and may have suffered low self-esteem. "Who am I that the pharaoh should listen to me?" He was a man with a momentous mission from God. The *Torah* testifies that he was the humblest person who ever lived. Moses successfully led Israel out of Egyptian slavery but he died just shy of entrance into the promised land.

Laozi did not exalt himself above anyone or anything, including birds, bees, beasts and blades of grass. The old sage claimed no credit for accomplishing anything. Laozi was as humble as dirt. In harmony with nature, he denounced civilization and exited society in mystical union with the *Dao*.

Confucius understood himself as an agent of Heaven but never considered himself to be anything more than a mortal man. He did not claim to create any institutions or author any original ideas. He identified himself as a lover of the ancients whom he believed possessed the solution for the salvation of society. Confucius died failing to see the fulfillment of his utopic vision.

Mahāvīra proclaimed himself to be a conqueror of *karma*; he believed that he had achieved supreme enlightenment of the true eternal self, endowed with original purity, unlimited self-awareness, infinite energy and unbounded bliss. He taught an arduous ascetic path of liberation from bondage to *karma* but did not claim to be able to deliver anyone but himself from its clutches.

Buddha believed himself to be a mere mortal who woke up to the problem and solution of suffering. He categorically denied being angelic or divine and vehemently declined to be worshiped. He taught that anyone could become a *buddha*, an awakened one. Buddha claimed that he blew out the flame of passion to overcome suffering and realize *nibbāna*. He did not present himself as anyone's savior from bondage, suffering, ignorance or craving; instead he saw himself as a teacher of the Middle Way but did not claim to be the way itself.

Kṛṣṇa claimed to be the supreme creator, sustainer and destroyer of all worlds. He proclaimed divine prerogative to grant his devotees liberation from bondage to *karma* by grace through exclusive, faithful devotion to him. He descends to earth to protect the virtuous, to destroy evil-doers, and to establish a firm basis for the true eternal order.

Jesus began his ministry by entering a synagogue and reading aloud from the scroll of *Isaiah* which plainly predicts the arrival of the *Messiah*.[52]

> The Spirit of the Lord is on me, because he has anointed me to proclaim good news to the poor. He has sent me to proclaim freedom for the prisoners and recovery of sight to the blind, to set the oppressed free, to proclaim the year of the Lord's favor.[53]

After reading it, Jesus declared to those present: "Today, this Scripture is fulfilled in your presence."[54]

When the disciples of John the Baptist asked Jesus directly whether he was the *Messiah*, Jesus told them to return to John and tell him that the blind are receiving their sight, the lame are walking, the deaf are hearing and the mute are talking, all prophetic signs of the *Messiah's* arrival.[55]

Throughout his public ministry, Jesus pronounced forgiveness of sins upon several of the people he healed. His presumption of the prerogative to forgive sin provoked the anger and indignation of the religious authorities who accused him of blasphemy because only God can forgive sin. After having pronounced forgiveness of sin to a paralytic, Jesus said to his accusers: "Which is easier to say, your sins are forgiven or get up and walk? So that all may know that I have authority to forgive sins, I command you: arise, pick up your mat, and walk."[56]

Jesus saw himself as the subordinate servant and Son of God, sent as a sacrifice to save sinners from slavery to sin. Jesus understood himself as the one and only *Messiah* sent to inaugurate the kingdom of God and to die and rise again to procure it. While each giant proposed plausible solutions to the particular problems they predicated, only Jesus promised to save people from sin. "You will know the truth and the truth will set you free."[57]

What Christians Might Learn From Jesus

From Jesus, Christians can learn to boldly bear testimony to the truth. All but one of the religious giants confronted in this work lived and died long before Jesus was born. Jesus may have heard about them. Ideas and artifacts traveled back and forth from China and India to Greece and the Middle East, reaching even to Jerusalem. In the face of conflicting and competing religious truth claims, Jesus said: "I am the way, the truth, and the life; no one comes to the father except by me."[58]

The gospel is universal and inclusive because it issues the same invitation to every tongue, tribe and nation. Jesus is peculiar but not parochial; he is the one for all. Jesus' way to God is narrow but wide open to everyone. The final words of the risen Jesus were delivered to his disciples in the context of rival world religions:

All authority in heaven and earth has been given to me. Go therefore and make disciples of all nations, baptizing them in the name of the Father, Son and Holy Spirit, and teach them to observe all that I have commanded you, and behold, I am with you always, even to the end of the world.[59]

Notes

1. Mark 3:21, *Holy Bible: New International Version*, Zondervan Publishers, 1984. All Bible references are based on this translation unless otherwise noted.
2. John 8:48.
3. Cassidy, Richard J., *Christians and Roman Rule in the New Testament: New Perspectives*, The Crossroad Publishing, 2001.
4. Crossan, John Dominic, *In the Shadow of the Empire: Reclaiming the Bible as a History of Faithful Resistance*, Westminster John Knox Press, 2008.
5. Matthew 11:29.
6. Horsley, Richard A., *Jesus and Empire: The Kingdom of God and the New World Disorder*, Augsburg Fortress Press, 2003.
7. Luke 1:3–4.
8. John 20:31.
9. Matthew 1:1–17.

10. *Ruth* 3.
11. *Matthew* 1:20.
12. Allen, William Cully, "Matthew's Genealogy of Jesus: A Seminal Study" in *Tattvanveshan*, Varanasi, India, 2015.
13. *Luke* 2:41–52.
14. *Luke* 2:48–49.
15. Prophet, Elizabeth Clare, *The Lost Years of Jesus: Documentary Evidence of Jesus' 17-year Journey to the East,* Summit Publications, 1984; Notovitch, Nicolas, *The Unknown Life of Jesus Christ,* Wilder Publications, 2008.
16. *Mark* 1:2–3.
17. *Matthew* 3:17.
18. *Luke* 16:16.
19. *Matthew* 4:1–11.
20. *Mark* 1:15.
21. *Mark* 4:11–12.
22. *Mark* 1:17.
23. *Mark* 1:24–25.
24. *Mark* 1:29–31.
25. *Mark* 1:32–34.
26. *Mark* 1:38.
27. *Mark* 2:17.
28. *Mark* 8:27–29.
29. *John* 6: 14–15.
30. *Mark* 8:31.
31. *Mark* 8:34.
32. *Mark* 9:7.
33. *Mark* 9:9.
34. *Mark* 9:31–32.
35. *Mark* 9:35–36.
36. *Mark* 10:32–34.
37. *Mark* 10:42–45.
38. *Mark* 11:9–10.
39. *Mark* 11:18.
40. *Mark* 14:2.
41. *Mark* 14:22–24.
42. *Mark* 14:41–42.
43. *Mark* 14:48–49.
44. *Mark* 14:61–65.
45. *Mark* 15:2–15.
46. *Mark* 15:17–20.
47. *Mark* 15:25.
48. *Mark* 15:43–47.
49. *Mark* 16:6–7.
50. *Mark* 16:15–16.

51. *Matthew* 18:36.
52. *Isaiah* 7:14.
53. *Luke* 4:18–19.
54. *Luke* 4:14–30.
55. *Luke* 7:20–23.
56. *Matthew* 9:5.
57. *John* 8:32.
58. *John* 14:6.
59. *Matthew* 28-18-20.

INDEX